A HANDBOOK

OF

PRÉCIS - WRITING

A HANDBOOK

OF

PRÉCIS-WRITING

WITH GRADUATED EXERCISES

by

E. DERRY EVANS

Cambridge :
at the University Press
1957

CAMBRIDGE UNIVERSITY PRESS
Cambridge, New York, Melbourne, Madrid, Cape Town,
Singapore, São Paulo, Delhi, Mexico City

Cambridge University Press
The Edinburgh Building, Cambridge CB2 8RU, UK

Published in the United States of America by Cambridge University Press, New York

www.cambridge.org
Information on this title: www.cambridge.org/9781107621145

First edition 1913
Reprinted 1916, 1921, 1924, 1929, 1933, 1939, 1950, 1957
First published 1957
First paperback edition 2013

A catalogue record for this publication is available from the British Library

ISBN 978-1-107-62114-5 Paperback

PREFACE

SEVERAL universities and examining boards have lately recognised the utility of Précis-writing, and the present volume has been compiled to meet what the writer considers is a long-felt want.

For several years, it has been a part of his duty to prepare candidates in English for the London Matriculation and the Senior Certificate of the Central Welsh Board, and as no suitable text-book appeared for a considerable time to meet the requirements of these examinations, it became necessary to select appropriate passages for this purpose from a wide range of English authors. The book is therefore the outcome of a long experience in teaching Précis-writing, and the majority of the pieces selected have been worked as exercises in a Matriculation form. While the book is intended mainly for candidates preparing for the above-mentioned Examinations, the author considers that this valuable exercise may with advantage be taken up earlier in the school-course, e.g., by forms preparing for the Junior Certificate of the Central Welsh Board, and all the passages in Part I have been carefully graded to make them suitable for pupils beginning the subject. It will be clear therefore that the present volume is not expressly intended for candidates preparing for such Examinations as those of the Civil Service and the Army, in which a large mass of official correspondence has to be summarised. At the same time, it is hoped that this handbook will afford the pupil such a sound training in the principles of précis-writing as will enable him to proceed to the more difficult branches of the subject with comparative ease.

It remains for me to acknowledge my obligations to various authorities for permission to print certain of the selections: to Sir John Stirling-Maxwell and to Messrs Blackie and Son, Ltd., for the extract from the late Sir William Stirling-Maxwell's speech; to the University of London for Nos. 54, 58; to the Central Welsh Board for Nos. 9, 11, 15, 47; to the Controller of H. M. Stationery Office for the extract from the Poor Law Commission Minority Report; to the editor of the *Manchester Guardian* for extract No. 60; to the Walter Scott Publishing Co. for the extract from their edition of Lowell's *My Study Windows*; and to Messrs Macmillan & Co. for extract No. 59 taken from Davies and Vaughan's translation of Plato's *Republic*.

I am also indebted to my friend and colleague Mr E. Morgan Williams, B.A., for several valuable suggestions.

E. D. E.

Towyn,
October, 1913.

CONTENTS

INTRODUCTION

Précis-writing, or the art of giving a concise and lucid summary of a lengthy passage of prose or poetry, is a valuable exercise and one that is frequently demanded in every business and in every profession. Next to Latin Prose Composition, it is the best means adapted for developing the power of penetration, of seizing upon the salient parts in a narrative, and expressing these in clear and vigorous speech. Whether the student is called upon to give the substance of a book, a sermon, a platform speech, or a public debate, a thorough training in précis-writing will teach him how to select everything that is of essential importance, and to discard whatever is irrelevant to the main theme, so that his summary may present the concentrated essence of what he has read or heard. It is therefore an excellent antidote to the far too prevalent habit of reading without attempting to obtain an accurate impression of the content.

How to set about writing a Précis.

The following directions have been found helpful and will repay careful study.

(1) The pupil should read the passage carefully through two or three times, consulting the dictionary for the meaning of difficult words, until he has a clear idea of its general purport. Great importance should be attached to this, for

until the gist of the passage is clearly grasped, it is useless to begin writing down the abstract.

(2) When he is satisfied as to the main theme, he should then consider the passage in detail. On careful reading he will find that the argument generally resolves itself into certain well-defined sections. He should observe carefully the connection between them and write down a suitable heading for each section.

(3) The next step is to select the points of importance that must be incorporated in the précis, and to exclude whatever is not essential to the subject of the original. And here the following caution cannot be too strongly emphasised. Most pupils are under the impression that it is sufficient to select at random a few detached sentences from the extract, and string these together without any attempt at continuity. Such results are useless. *The pupil must bear in mind that the one all-important rule in précis-writing is that his summary must present an intelligible account of the substance of the original to a person who has not the original to consult.* Hence, as it is only the concentrated essence of the original that must be retained, he should note carefully :

(*a*) No additional matter is to be inserted by way of personal comment or historical explanation.

(*b*) All superfluous details such as long quotations or lengthy enumerations, added merely to illustrate the argument, must be omitted. For instance in Exercise 38, Part II, he must not enumerate the various countries or recount the different reforms mentioned by Macaulay in his sketch of the progress of England. Rhetorical figures of speech such as metaphors, similes, and personifications will also disappear.

(*c*) Poetical passages, which usually abound in figurative expressions require careful consideration; for while poetical ornament is generally to be excluded, the diction must not be so bald as to be entirely shorn of the dignity of the original.

(4) When the process of selection and elimination is finished, the pupil should now proceed to weave the various ideas into a concise and lucid narrative. To do this effectively requires considerable experience in the use of felicitous and comprehensive terms. It is also advisable to construct a *preliminary* draft of the précis, taking care at this stage that all the salient points of the original are incorporated.

(5) Further, the narrative will not be lucid unless the principle of continuity is observed. It is not sufficient that the sentences should express the ideas of the different sections as *briefly* as possible, but they must also follow each other in logical sequence, and be welded together by means of suitable connectives into a vigorous and organic whole.

When the first draft is completed, the pupil should carefully read it through, when he will probably find that further condensation is possible, before the *final* draft is written.

(6) *Length of Précis.* No hard and fast rule can be laid down as to the relative length of a précis, as extracts differ considerably in their structure and content. In practice, however, it will be found that the majority of the short passages in Part I of this book, can be reduced to about one-third of the original, while the substance of most of the longer passages in Parts II and III should be expressed in about one-fifth of their present length.

(7) *Tense and Person.* In the Exercises contained in this book the *tense* of the original should remain unchanged except in the extracts from Shakespeare and No. 59, Part III. (In the case, however, of complicated correspondence, such as is usually set at Civil Service Examinations, the incidents described refer to the past, and therefore the past tense should be used throughout.)

It is advisable that the third person should be used in précis-writing, unless it is found that the form of the original extract does not admit of its being converted into indirect speech.

(8) Finally, the cardinal requirements of a good précis may be summed up in three words: clearness, coherence, brevity, and the greatest of these is clearness.

A few typical examples of varied difficulty are here discussed and a model précis appended to each in order to illustrate the application of the above directions.

Example I.

No degree of knowledge attainable by man is able to set him above the want of hourly assistance, or to extinguish the desire of fond endearments and tender officiousness : and therefore no one should think it unnecessary to learn those arts by which friendship may be gained.   Kindness is preserved by a constant reciprocation of benefits or interchange of pleasures; but such benefits only can be bestowed as others are capable to receive, and such pleasures only imparted, as others are qualified to enjoy.

Dr JOHNSON, Rambler.

The main purport of the passage is :

The preservation of friendship.

The piece divides itself naturally into two paragraphs ; the first extending as far as "gained"; and the second from "Kindness" to the end.

The main purport of each paragraph respectively is:

(1)   The offices of friendship are indispensable.

(2)   How to preserve friendship.

The précis of the whole will be :

As the services of friends are indispensable even to men of the highest intellectual attainments, we should cultivate friendship by the interchange of such kindnesses as are mutually acceptable.

Example II.

Enter SHYLOCK

Duke. Make room and let him stand before our face:
Shylock, the world thinks and I think so too,
That thou but lead'st this fashion of thy malice
To the last hour of act; and then 'tis thought
Thou 'lt show thy mercy and remorse more strange
Than is thy strange apparent cruelty;
And where thou now exact'st the penalty,
Which is a pound of this poor merchant's flesh,
Thou wilt not only loose the forfeiture,
But, touched with human gentleness and love
Forgive a moiety of the principal;
Glancing an eye of pity on his losses,
That have of late so huddled on his back,
Enough to press a royal merchant down
And pluck commiseration of his state
From brassy bosoms and rough hearts of flint,
From stubborn Turks and Tartars, never trained
To offices of tender courtesy.
We all expect a gentle answer, Jew.

Shylock. I have possess'd your grace of what I purpose,
And by our holy Sabbath have I sworn
To have the due and forfeit of my bond:
If you deny it, let the danger light
Upon your charter, and your city's freedom.
You 'll ask me, why I rather choose to have
A weight of carrion flesh than to receive
Three thousand ducats: I 'll not answer that:

Example II.

The title of the whole passage will be:

Shylock's defence before the Duke.

In passages like the above, the tendency of most pupils is to construct the précis in the form of a dialogue in the first person, giving a separate summary of what is spoken by each person. This method should be avoided. The substance of the several speeches should be combined into one continuous narrative, written in the third person.

The dialogue comprises two sections. The last six lines of the Duke's speech, as the pupil will readily see, add nothing that is essential to the substance of the passage, and may, therefore, be omitted in the précis. The prominent idea is the Duke's appeal to Shylock to waive his claim to the forfeit, and remit a portion of the original loan. The heading for this section is therefore:

The Duke's appeal to Shylock for mercy.

Shylock's reply is considerably more difficult to summarise. Particular mention must not be made in the précis of the various animals, and the feelings of dislike they engender in different persons, but these details must be summarised by means of some comprehensive phrase. The main ideas are (*a*) Shylock's refusal; (*b*) the explanation of his hatred for Antonio. The heading for this section therefore may be expressed thus:

Shylock's refusal and his explanation.

Example II. (continued)

> But say it is my humour: is it answer'd?
> What if my house be troubled with a rat,
> And I be pleas'd to give ten thousand ducats
> To have it baned? What, are you answer'd yet?
> Some men there are love not a gaping pig;
> Some that are mad if they behold a cat;
> And others at the bagpipe; for affection,
> Mistress of passion, sways it to the mood
> Of what it likes or loathes. Now for your answer:
> As there is no firm reason to be render'd
> Why he cannot abide a gaping pig;
> Why he, a harmless necessary cat;
> Why he, a woollen bagpipe;
> So can I give no reason, nor I will not
> More than a lodg'd hate and a certain loathing
> I bear Antonio, that I follow thus
> A losing suit against him. Are you answer'd?
>
> SHAKESPERE, *Merchant of Venice.*

9

Example II. (continued)

Bearing in mind therefore the above directions, we shall express our final précis somewhat as follows:

Addressing Shylock, the Duke expressed the general expectation that he would at the last moment waive his claim to the pound of flesh, and moreover, out of consideration for the merchant's heavy losses would remit a portion of the original loan. Shylock, in reply, insisted on the execution of the bond, adding that such strange idiosyncrasies as the instinctive dislike felt by some towards certain animals were inexplicable, and of such a nature was his antipathy to Antonio.

Example III.

Lift—lift ye mists, from off the silent coast
   Folded in endless winter's chill embraces;
Unshroud for us awhile our brave ones lost;
   Let us behold their faces:

In vain: the North has hid them from our sight;
   The snow their winding sheet—their only dirges,
The groan of icebergs in the Polar night,
   Racked by the savage surges.

No funeral torches, which a smoky glare
   Shone a farewell upon their shrouded faces;
No monumental pillar tall and fair,
   Towers o'er their resting places.

But northern streamers flare the long night through
   Over the cliffs stupendous, fraught with peril,
Of icebergs, tinted with a ghostly hue
   Of amethyst and beryl.

No human tears upon their graves are shed—
   Tears of domestic love or pity holy;
But snowflakes from the gloomy sky o'erhead
   Down shuddering, settle slowly.

Yet history shrines them with her mighty dead,
   The hero seamen of this isle of Britain;
And, when the brighter scroll of Heaven is read
   There will their names be written.

       HOOD, *The Lost Expedition with Franklin.*

Example III.

In this beautiful elegiac poem from Thomas Hood, our greatest difficulty will be to preserve something of the pathos and dignity of the poetry. To effect this, it may be necessary for the précis to be somewhat longer in comparison with the original than in the case of a prose passage, for it is easier to "dissect a worm than a butterfly." The many poetical figures in which the piece abounds must not appear, and the fourth stanza, which refers to the Aurora Borealis, may be entirely omitted. The ideas that emerge most prominently after a careful analysis are:

(1) The futility of our yearning for the lost heroes.

(2) The inaccessible nature of their last resting-place.

(3) The absence of all tokens of commemoration.

(4) Their imperishable fame.

The final précis will be:

All vain is our yearning for the brave band who perished in the attempt to discover the North-West passage, for their bodies lie buried among the snows and perilous icebergs of the Polar regions. Though their graves are not marked by any commemorative tablet, or token of affection, their names will ever be recorded on the scroll of Britain's immortal heroes.

Example IV.

The inhabitants of towns having been declared free by the Charters of communities, that part of the people which resided in the country and was employed in agriculture, began to recover liberty by enfranchisement. During the rigour of feudal government, as hath already been observed, the great body of the lower people was reduced to servitude. They were always fixed to the soil which they cultivated, and together with it were transferred from one proprietor to another, by sale or by conveyance. The spirit of feudal policy did not favour the enfranchisement of that order of men. It was an established maxim that no vassal could legally diminish the value of a fief to the detriment of the lord from whom he received it. In consequence of this, manumission by the authority of the immediate master was not valid; and unless it was confirmed by the immediate lord of whom he held, slaves belonging to the fief did not acquire a complete right to their liberty. Thus it became necessary to ascend through all the gradations of feudal holding to the King, the lord paramount. A form of procedure so tedious and troublesome discouraged the practice of manumission. Domestic or personal slaves often obtained liberty from the humanity or beneficence of their masters, to whom they belonged in absolute property The condition of slaves fixed to the soil was much more unalterable.

But the freedom and independence which one part of the people had obtained by the institution of communities inspired the other with the most ardent desire of acquiring the same privileges; and their superiors, sensible of the various advantages which they had derived from their former concessions to their dependents, were less unwilling to gratify them by the grant of new immunities. The enfranchisement of slaves became more frequent; and the monarchs of France, prompted by necessity no less than by their own inclination to reduce the power of the nobles, endeavoured to render it general. Louis X and Philip the Long issued ordinances declaring "that all men were by nature free born, and as their Kingdom was called the Kingdom

Example IV.

From a careful analysis of the above passage we shall find that it may be divided into four sections: the first extending from the beginning to "conveyance"; the second from " The spirit of feudal policy " to " unalterable"; the third from " But the freedom " to " Kingdom " and the fourth from " The effects of such a remarkable change " to the end. In the first section the student will notice that the gist of the first sentence is expressed at the beginning of the third section; hence for the purpose of our précis, these two sentences will be combined. The heading of the first part will obviously be:

> *The servile condition of villeins under the*
> *feudal system.*

In the second section, the prominent idea is the difficulty of obtaining liberty for the villein. It will not be necessary to give a detailed description of the process of manumission demanded by the laws of feudal tenure; it will be sufficient for our purpose to refer to this in general terms. The comparison at the end between domestic slaves and villeins bound to the soil, is not vital to the substance of the passage, and therefore it may be omitted. The heading for the second section is therefore:

> *The difficulty of obtaining manumission.*

The third section describes the causes that led to the abolition of servitude, and as these are important, they must be carefully noted. They are (*a*) the advantages accruing from the enfranchisement of townsmen by charter, and (*b*) the noble example set by the French Kings in emancipating their subjects. The general heading for the section will be:

> *Causes leading to the emancipation of the peasantry.*

Example IV. (continued)

of Franks, they determined that it should be so in reality as well as in name ; therefore they appointed that enfranchisements should be granted throughout the whole Kingdom upon just and honourable conditions." These edicts were carried into immediate execution within the Royal domain. The example of their Sovereigns, together with the expectation of considerable sums which they might raise by this expedient, led many of the Nobles to set their dependents at liberty ; and servitude was gradually abolished in almost every province in the Kingdom. The effects of such a remarkable change in the condition of so great a part of the people could not fail of being considerable and extensive. The husbandman, master of his own industry and secure of reaping for himself the fruits of his labour, became the farmer of the same fields where he had formerly been compelled to toil for the benefit of another. The odious names of master and of slave were abolished. New prospects opened, and new incitements to ingenuity and enterprise presented themselves to those who were emancipated. The expectation of bettering their fortune as well as that of raising themselves to a more honourable condition, concurred in calling forth their activity and genius ; and a numerous class of men who formerly had no political existence, became useful citizens, and contributed towards augmenting the force of riches of the society which adopted them as members.

Robertson, *History of the Reign of Charles V.*

Example IV. (continued)

The first sentence in the fourth section gives a clear indication of its contents. Broadly speaking the results of emancipation are two : (*a*) New incentives to enterprise given to the husbandman, and (*b*) The increase in the number of useful citizens.

Heading for this section:

Beneficial results of emancipation.

We are now in a position to write down the title of the whole passage, viz.:

The emancipation of the peasantry.

Précis of the whole :

Under the feudal system tillers of the soil were reduced to servitude, and as they could only be enfranchised by a tedious process, the practice of manumission was discouraged. But the advantages derived from the enfranchisement of townsmen, and the example set by the French Kings of emancipating their serfs led to the gradual abolition of the servitude of villeins.

Such a reform inspired the husbandman to greater enterprise, and increased the number of citizens who contributed to the welfare of the state.

In the following Exercises, the pupil is requested :

(1) To select (*a*) a suitable title or heading for each exercise, (*b*) the particular subject of each paragraph.

(2) To write a précis of the passage without anything superfluous.

PART I

EASY

1

A drop of water fell out of a cloud into the sea, and finding itself lost in such an immensity of fluid matter, broke out into the following reflection : " Alas ! what an inconsiderable creature am I in this prodigious ocean of waters : My existence is of no concern in the universe ; I am reduced to a kind of nothing, and am less than the least of the works of God." It so happened that an oyster which lay in the neighbourhood of this drop chanced to gape and swallow it up in the midst of this his humble soliloquy. The drop, says the fable, lay a great while hardening in the shell, until by degrees it was ripened into a pearl, which, falling into the hands of a diver, after a long series of adventures, is at present that famous pearl which is fixed on the top of the Persian diadem.

ADDISON, *The Spectator.*

2

A painter of eminence was once resolved to finish a piece which should please the whole world. When, therefore, he had drawn a picture, in which his utmost skill was exhausted, it was exposed in the public market-place, with directions at the bottom for every spectator to mark with a brush, which lay by, every limb and feature which seemed erroneous. The spectators came, and in general applauded ; but each, willing to show his talent at criticism, marked whatever he thought proper. At evening, when the painter came, he was mortified to find the whole picture one universal blot—not a single stroke that was not stigmatized with marks of disapprobation: not satisfied with this trial, the next day he was resolved to try them in a different manner, and, exposing his picture as before, desired that every spectator would mark those beauties he approved or admired. The people complied; and the artist returning, found his picture replete with the marks of beauty: every stroke that had been yesterday condemned, now received the character of approbation. "Well," cries the painter, "I now find that the best way to please one half of the world is not to mind what the other half says; since what are faults in the eyes of these, shall be by those regarded as beauties."

GOLDSMITH, *The Citizen of the World.*

3

The pilgrims by-and-by saw a town before them, and the name of that town is Vanity; and at the town there is a fair kept, called Vanity Fair. It is kept all the year round. The pilgrims had no choice but to go through this fair. But, as soon as they entered the fair, all the people in the fair were roused, and the town itself, it seemed, into a hubbub about them. For they were clothed differently from all that traded in that fair; and they spoke a different language, the language of Canaan; and they set very little value upon all the wares in the fair. It happened that one of the sellers of goods said mockingly to the pilgrims, "What will you buy?" But they looked gravely at him, and said, "We buy the truth." Thereupon occasion was taken to abuse the men the more; some mocking, some taunting, some speaking reproachfully, and some calling upon others to smite them. At last things came to a hubbub and a great commotion in the fair, so that the fair became simply a confused crowd. Then word was sent at once to the master of the fair, who quickly came down and deputed some of his trusted friends to examine those men who had nearly turned the fair into a mob. So the men were brought before these judges; and they asked from

what place they came, whither they were bound, and what they
were doing there in such a strange place. The men told them
that they were pilgrims and strangers in the world, and that they
were going to their own country, which was the heavenly Jerusa-
lem. But those that were appointed to examine them did not
believe them to be anything but lunatics and madmen, or else
such as came to raise disturbance in the fair. Therefore they
took them and beat them, and besmeared them with dirt, and
then put them into the cage, that they might be made a spectacle
to all the men of the fair.   BUNYAN, *Pilgrim's Progress.*

4

Upon a time, unbidden, came a man
Before the mighty King of Teberistan.
When the King saw this daring man, he cried,
"Who art thou, fellow?" Whereto he replied,
"A lion-hunter and a swordsman, I,
Moreover, I am skilled in archery:
A famous bowman, who of men alone
Can drive his arrows through the hardest stone.
Besides my courage, tried in desperate wars,
I know to read the riddle of the stars.
First in the service of Emeer Khojend,
Who, friend of none, has none to be his friend—
Him have I left, I hope, an honest man,
To serve if so he wills the Lord of Teberistan."
To whom in answer: "I have men enow,
Stalwart like thee, apt with the sword and bow;
These no King lacks, or need to; what we need
Are men who may be trusted—word and deed:
Who to keep pain from us would yield their breath;
Faithful in life, and faithfuller in death."
"Try me." As thrice the monarch claps his hands,
The Captain of the guard before him stands,

Amazed that one, unknown to him, had come
In to the King, and fearful of his doom.
Sternly his lord: "You guard me, slave, so well
That I have made this man my sentinel."
Thus did the happy archer gain his end,
And thus his sovereign find at last a friend,
Who from that hour was to his service bound
Keen as his hawk, and faithful as his hound.

An Eastern Legend.

5

The elephant is very nervous, like almost all wild animals, and is easily startled by a sudden or unexpected noise. Instances are known where a man has been in great danger among a herd of wild elephants, and has saved himself by suddenly clapping his hands, by which action the animals were so startled that the man was enabled to escape and hide himself during their fright. A strange object also alarms an elephant exceedingly, and will frequently disturb his equanimity of mind.

All elephants have a great dislike to little animals, or animals that are little in comparison with themselves. In hunting, the elephants like to avoid the dogs, and evince great uneasiness if they hear the dogs following them. But nothing appears to discompose an elephant more than being followed by a horse, especially if it is going at a quick pace. The clatter of the hoofs seems to alarm elephants considerably even when they see the horse, but their fear is increased when the sound comes from behind them. There are some animals which the elephant cannot endure, even when they are quiet. The tiger is one of these creatures; and there is good reason for this dislike; but why elephants should refuse to approach a camel is not quite so clear. The elephant will travel in company with camels when they are laden without exhibiting much repugnance, but it does not like to come near a camel which has no burden.

Wood, *Anecdotes of Animal Life.*

2—2

6

I lay down on the grass, which was very short and soft, where I slept sounder than ever I remember to have done in my life. I attempted to rise, but was not able to stir; for as I happened to lie on my back, I found my arms and legs were strongly fastened on each side to the ground, and my hair, which was long and thick, tied down in the same manner. I heard a confused noise about me, but in the posture I lay, could see nothing except the sky. In a little time I felt something alive moving on my left leg, which advancing gently forward over my breast, came almost up to my chin: when bending my eyes downwards as much as I could, I perceived it to be a human creature not six inches high, with a bow and arrow in his hands, and a quiver at his back. In the meantime, I felt at least forty more of the same kind, (as I conjectured) following the first. I was in the utmost astonishment and roared so loud, that they all ran back in a fright; and some of them, as I was afterwards told, were hurt with the falls they got by leaping from my sides upon the ground. I lay all this while in great uneasiness; at length, struggling to get loose, I had the fortune to break the strings, and wrench out the pegs that fastened my left arm to the ground; and at the same time with a violent pull, which gave me excessive pain, I'd a little loosened the strings that tied down my hair on the left side, so that I was just able to turn my head about two inches. But the creatures ran off a second time, before I could seize them. With a great shout in a very shrill accent, they discharged about an hundred arrows on my left hand, which pricked me like so many needles. When this shower of arrows was over, I fell a groaning with grief and pain, and then striving again to get loose, they discharged another volley, larger than the first, and some of them attempted with spears to stick me in the sides; but by good luck, I had on me a buff jerkin which they could not pierce. I thought it the most prudent method to lie still. And when the people observed I was quiet, they discharged no more arrows.

SWIFT, *Gulliver's Travels*.

7

Eugenius is a man of universal good-nature, and generous beyond the extent of his fortune; but withal so prudent in the economy of his affairs, that what goes out in charity is made up by good management. Eugenius has what the world calls two hundred pounds a year; but never values himself above nine score, as not thinking he has a right to the tenth part, which he always appropriates to charitable uses. To this sum he frequently makes other voluntary additions, insomuch that in a good year, for such he accounts those in which he has been able to make greater bounties than ordinary, he has given above twice the sum to the sickly and indigent. Eugenius prescribes to himself many particular days of fasting and abstinence, in order to increase his private bank of charity, and sets aside what would be the current expenses of those times for the poor. He often goes afoot where his business calls him, and at the end of his walk has given a shilling, which in his ordinary methods of expense would have gone for coach-hire, to the first necessitous person that has fallen in his way. I have known him, when he has been going to a play or an opera, divert the money which was designed for that purpose, upon an object of charity whom he has met with in the street; and afterwards pass his evening in a coffee-house, or at a friend's fireside, with much greater satisfaction to himself than he could have received from the most exquisite entertainments of the theatre. By these means he is generous without impoverishing himself, and enjoys his estate by making it the property of others. ADDISON, *The Spectator.*

8

The deep affections of the breast,
That Heaven to living things imparts,
Are not exclusively possessed
By human hearts.

A parrot from the Spanish main
   Full young and early caged, came o'er
With bright wings to the bleak domain
   Of Mulla's[1] shore.

To spicy groves, where he had won
   This plumage of resplendent hue,
His native fruits, and skies and sun,
   He bade adieu.

For these he changed the smoke of turf,
   A heathery land, and misty sky,
And turned on rocks and raging surf
   His golden eye.

But petted, in our climate cold
   He lived and chattered many a day,
Until with age from green and gold
   His wings grew grey.

At last, when blind and seeming dumb
   He scolded, laughed, and spoke no more,
A Spanish stranger chanced to come
   To Mulla's shore.

He hailed the bird in Spanish speech,
   The bird in Spanish speech replied,
Flapped round his cage with joyous screech,
   Dropt down and died.   CAMPBELL.

[1] Mulla. The island of Mull on the west coast of Scotland.

9

Pygmalion was a sculptor who lived in the island of Cyprus. For many years he had worked with great labour, and at last he could use the chisel with a mas'er's hand. The figures that he carved from senseless blocks of marble and wood, were so perfect, that some who came to look at them, really were deceived, and thought that living men and women stood before them. And yet Pygmalion himself was not satisfied with what he had done. He still wished to do something better, so he wrought a statue of snow-white ivory in the form of a beautiful woman. He gave himself no rest till this was done; all the best thoughts of his mind, and all the cunning that his hand possessed, had been used to create the form which now stood before him. You might almost say that he had put part of his own life into it.

Pygmalion himself began to admire the statue more and more, and to imagine that it was indeed like one alive. He was almost afraid, that if he touched it roughly, a mark would be left just as if he had grasped a living arm.

Then he began to hang trinkets and jewels on the lovely statue, and to slip rings on her fingers, and to talk to her as if she were alive. Silks too he bought to clothe her limbs, and flowers of many hues he laid at her feet.

Nevertheless, he knew full well in his heart, that she was only a statue, since she could neither breathe nor speak. But he desired so much that the lovely form should answer when he spoke to her, that at last he went into the temple, and entreated the gods that the ivory statue might really live. Then he went home, doubting much that this could ever come to pass; but when he opened the door and looked within, he saw no longer a silent statue, but a living maiden who both breathed and spoke!

Thereupon Pygmalion was so much amazed, that he could hardly believe it to be true. But when at length he took courage to come nearer, and saw that her cheeks were red, and her eyes bright and shining, and when too she told him that she loved him, then the sculptor knew that the gods had answered his prayer, and he rejoiced greatly, and made the maiden his wife.

Central Welsh Board Junior Certificate, 1908.

24

10

There is another way of reasoning which seldom fails, though it be of a quite different nature to that I have last mentioned. I mean, convincing a man by ready money, or, as it is ordinarily called, bribing a man to an opinion. This method has often proved successful, when all the others have been made use of to no purpose. A man who is furnished with arguments from the mint, will convince the antagonist much sooner than one who draws them from reason and philosophy. Gold is a wonderful clearer of the understanding; it dissipates every doubt and scruple in an instant; accommodates itself to the meanest capacities; silences the loud and clamorous, and brings over the most obstinate and inflexible. Philip of Macedon was a man of most invincible reason this way. He refuted by it all the wisdom of Athens, confounded their statesmen, struck their orators dumb, and at length argued them out of all their liberties.

ADDISON, *The Spectator.*

11

No one can doubt that it is the duty of men and women to think not of their own interests, but of the interests of those who are dependent upon them; that is, of the interests of their families. But our country is only the great family to which we all belong. Men and women, then, should remember that it is their duty to think of the interests of their country, and should put these interests above all others. We must not imagine, however, that by caring about our country, and thinking what is best for it, we shall run any risk of neglecting the interests of our families, or of ourselves. If we rightly understand our duty to ourselves and our families, and do that duty, we shall at the same time be doing our duty to the mother of us all—our country.

When Nelson spoke to the sailors of the English fleet just before a great battle, the words he used were: " England expects every man to do his duty." The words are just as true for the ordinary world, and for the common everyday battle of life in which we all have to fight. Our country expects every man to do his duty, whether he lives in England, Scotland, Wales, or Ireland. But in the interests of his country, of his family, and of himself, a man's first duty is to make the best of himself—that is, to make the best use of the powers of body and powers of mind with which he is born, and of the opportunities for using the powers which come in his way.

It is easy to see, that if men and women are to make the best of themselves, they must begin when they are boys and girls to plan how they shall do it. The first and most important way of making the best of ourselves is doing the work that suits us best. As we have all to work in some way or other, it is of great importance that we should work at what we can do well.

Central Welsh Board Junior Certificate, 1901.

12

The Luddites seem to have been encouraged by the lenity of the sentences pronounced on such of their confederates as had been apprehended and tried ; and shortly after, the mania broke out afresh, and rapidly extended over the northern and midland manufacturing districts. The organisation became more secret ; an oath was administered to the members binding them to obedience to the orders issued by the heads of the confederacy ; and the betrayal of their designs was decreed to be death. All machines were doomed by them to destruction, whether employed in the manufacture of cloth, calico, or lace ; and a reign of terror began which lasted for years. In Yorkshire and Lancashire, mills were boldly attacked by armed rioters, and in many cases they were wrecked or burnt; so that it became necessary to guard them by soldiers and yeomanry. The masters themselves were doomed to death ; many of them were assaulted, and some were murdered. At length the law was vigorously set in motion ;

numbers of the misguided Luddites were apprehended; some were executed; and after several years' violent commotion from this cause, the machine-breaking riots were at length quelled.

SMILES, *Self Help.*

13

Three fishers went sailing out into the West,
    Out into the West, as the sun went down;
Each thought on the woman who loved him the best,
    And the children stood watching them out of the town.
For men must work, and women must weep,
And there's little to earn, and many to keep,
    Though the harbour bar be moaning.

Three wives sat up in the lighthouse-tower,
    And they trimmed their lamps as the sun went down;
They looked at the squall, and they looked at the shower,
    And the night-rack came rolling up ragged and brown;
But men must work, and women must weep,
Though storms be sudden, and waters deep,
    And the harbour bar be moaning.

Three corpses lay out on the shining sands,
    In the morning gleam, as the tide went down,
And the women are weeping and wringing their hands
    For those who will never come back to the town.
For men must work, and women must weep,
And the sooner it's over, the sooner to sleep,
    And goodbye to the bar and its moaning.

C. KINGSLEY.

14

I remember last winter there were several young girls of the neighbourhood sitting about the fire with my landlady's daughters, and telling stories of spirits and apparitions. Upon my opening the door, the young women broke off their discourse, but my landlady's daughters telling them that it was nobody but the Gentleman, (for that is the name that I go by in the neighbourhood as well as in the family,) they went on without minding me. I seated myself by the candle that stood on a table at one end of the room ; and pretending to read a book that I took out of my pocket, heard several dreadful stories of ghosts as pale as ashes, that had stood at the feet of a bed, or walked over a churchyard by moonlight ; and of others that had been conjured into the Red Sea, for disturbing people's rest, and drawing their curtains at midnight ; with many other old women's fables of the like nature. As one spirit raised another, I observed that at the end of every story the whole company closed their ranks, and crowded about the fire. I took notice in particular of a little boy, who was so attentive to every story, that I am mistaken if he ventures to go to bed by himself this twelvemonth. Indeed they talked so long, that the imaginations of the whole assembly were manifestly crazed, and I am sure will be the worse for it as long as they live. I heard one of the girls, that had looked upon me over her shoulder, asking the company how long I had been in the room, and whether I did not look paler than I used to do. This put me under some apprehensions that I should be forced to explain myself, if I did not retire ; for which reason I took the candle in my hand, and went up into my chamber, not without wondering at this unaccountable weakness in reasonable creatures, that they should love to astonish and terrify one another.

ADDISON, *The Spectator.*

15

The number of the English had by this time dwindled to less than 10,000 men. They were, moreover, enfeebled by sickness and fatigue. But one and all shared the undaunted spirit of their leader, though fully conscious of the peril of their position. Both armies halted for the night within a short distance of each other. The English passed the time in prayerful meditation, and in fitting preparation for the morrow. Their opponents, fresh and confident, merrily beguiled the hours in playing dice; their stakes being the prisoners they anticipated taking in battle. By daybreak, each army had taken up its position. That of the English was admirably chosen; it was in a narrow field which the enemy could approach only in front, the flanks of the army being protected by hedges and thickets. Mindful of what had happened at Crecy and Poitiers, the French hesitated to attack; and some hours were passed in a state of inactivity on both sides. At length, Henry gave the order to advance. His archers planting in the ground the stakes with which they were provided, ran forward and discharged shower after shower of arrows with deadly effect; and when pressed by the French cavalry, retired for protection behind their palisade of stakes. The horses of the enemy, afflicted with innumerable wounds, became restive and unmanageable, and spread disorder through the ranks. The narrowness of the space in which they were confined, cramped their movements, and deprived them of the advantage of superior numbers. The confusion increased, and Henry, seizing the right moment, advanced with his men-at-arms upon the helpless and struggling mass. The carnage was terrible; the discomfiture of the enemy complete. More than 10,000 of them perished, including the flower of the nobility. Of the English there fell only 1600.

Central Welsh Board Junior Certificate, 1903.

16

The Basques are a singing rather than a poetical people. Notwithstanding the facility with which their tongue lends itself to the composition of verse, they have never produced among them a poet with the slightest pretensions to reputation ; but their voices are singularly sweet, and they are known to excel in musical composition. It is the opinion of a certain author, the Abbé D'Ilharce, who has written about them, that they derived the name *Cantabri*, by which they were known to the Romans, from *Khantor-ber*, signifying sweet singers. They possess much music of their own, some of which is said to be exceedingly ancient. Of this music specimens were published at Donostian (San Sebastian) in the year 1826, edited by a certain Juan Ignacio Iztueta. These consist of wild and thrilling marches, to the sound of which it is believed that the ancient Basques were in the habit of descending from their mountains to combat with the Romans, and subsequently with the Moors. While listening to them, it is easy to suppose oneself in the close vicinity of some desperate encounter. We seem to hear the charge of cavalry on the sounding plain, the clash of swords, and the rushing of men down the gorges of hills. This music is accompanied with words, but such words ! nothing can be imagined more stupid, common-place, and uninteresting. So far from being martial, they relate to every-day incidents, and appear to have no connection whatever with the music. They are evidently of modern date.

BORROW, *Bible in Spain.*

17

In a community of hunters and shepherds, every man easily and necessarily becomes a soldier. His ordinary avocations are perfectly compatible with all the duties of military service. However remote may be the expedition on which he is bound, he finds it easy to transport with him the stock from which he derives his subsistence. The whole people is an army ; the whole year a march. Such was the state of society which facilitated the gigantic conquests of Attila and Tamerlane.

But a people which subsists by the cultivation of the earth is in a very different situation. The husbandman is bound to the soil on which he labours. A long campaign would be ruinous to him. Still his pursuits are such as give to his frame both the active and the passive strength necessary to a soldier. Nor do they, at least in the infancy of agricultural science, demand his uninterrupted attention. At particular times of the year, he is almost wholly unemployed, and can, without injury to himself, afford the time necessary for a short expedition. Thus the legions of Rome were supplied during its earlier wars. The season during which the fields did not require the presence of the cultivators sufficed for a short inroad and a battle. These operations, too frequently interrupted to produce decisive results, yet served to keep up among the people a degree of discipline and courage which rendered them not only secure, but formidable.

MACAULAY, *Historical Essays.*

18

The death of Nelson was felt in England as something more than a public calamity: men started at the intelligence, and turned pale, as if they had heard of the loss of a dear friend. An object of our admiration and affection, of our pride and of our hopes, was suddenly taken from us; and it seemed as if we had never, till then, known how deeply we loved and reverenced him. What the country had lost in its great naval hero, the greatest of our own, and of all former times, was scarcely taken into the account of grief. So perfectly, indeed, had he performed his part, that the maritime war, after the battle of Trafalgar, was considered at an end: the fleets of the enemy were not merely defeated, but destroyed: new navies must be built, and a new race of seamen reared for them, before the possibility of their invading our shores could again be contemplated. It was not, therefore, from any selfish reflection upon the magnitude of our

loss that we mourned for him : the general sorrow was of a higher
character. The people of England grieved that funeral cere-
monies and public monuments, and posthumous rewards were all
that they could now bestow upon him, whom the King, the
legislature, and the nation, would have alike delighted to honour;
whom every tongue would have blessed ; whose presence in every
village through which he might have passed would have wakened
the Church bells, have given schoolboys a holiday, have drawn
children from their sports to gaze upon him, and "old men from
the chimney corner," to look upon Nelson ere they died. The
victory of Trafalgar was celebrated indeed, with the usual forms
of rejoicing, but they were without joy, for such already was the
glory of the British Navy, through Nelson's surpassing genius,
that it scarcely seemed to receive any addition from the most
signal victory that ever was achieved upon the seas : and the
destruction of the mighty fleet, by which all the maritime schemes
of France were totally frustrated, hardly appeared to add to our
security or strength ; for while Nelson was living to watch the
combined squadrons of the enemy, we felt ourselves as secure as
now, when they were no longer in existence.

SOUTHEY, *Life of Nelson.*

19

Life had been long astir in the village, and clamorous labour
Knocked with its hundred hands at the golden gates of the
  morning.
Now from the country around, from the farms and neighbouring
  hamlets,
Came in their holiday dresses the blithe Acadian peasants.
Many a glad good-morrow, and jocund laugh from the young folk
Made the bright air brighter, as up from the numerous meadows,
Where no path could be seen but the track of wheels in the
  greensward,
Group after group appeared, and joined, or passed on the
  highway.

Long ere noon, in the village all sounds of labour were silenced.
Thronged were the streets with people; and noisy groups at
    the house-doors
Sat in the cheerful sun, and rejoiced and gossiped together.
Every house was an inn, where all were welcomed and feasted;
For with this simple people, who lived like brothers together,
All things were held in common, and what one had was another's.
Yet under Benedict's roof hospitality seemed more abundant:
For Evangeline stood among the guests of her father;
Bright was her face with smiles, and words of welcome and
    gladness
Fell from her beautiful lips, and blessed the cup as she gave it.
Under the open sky, in the odorous air of the orchard,
Stript of its golden fruit, was spread the feast of betrothal.

LONGFELLOW, Evangeline.

20

    Foremost in the list of the benefits which our country owes to
the Revolution we place the Toleration Act. It is true that this
measure fell short of the wishes of the leading Whigs. It is
true also that, where Catholics were concerned, even the most
enlightened of the leading Whigs held opinions by no means
so liberal as those which are happily common at the present day.
Those distinguished statesmen did however make a noble, and,
in some respects, a successful struggle for the rights of conscience.
Their wish was to bring the great body of the Protestant Dissen-
ters within the pale of the Church by judicious alterations in the
Liturgy and the Articles, and to grant to those who still remained
without that pale the most ample toleration. They framed a plan
of comprehension which would have satisfied a great majority of
the seceders; and they proposed the complete abolition of that
absurd and odious test which, after having been, during a century
and a half, a scandal to the pious and a laughing-stock to the
profane, was at length removed in our own time. The immense
power of the Clergy and of the Tory gentry frustrated these

excellent designs. The Whigs, however, did much. They succeeded in obtaining a law in the provisions of which a philosopher will doubtless find much to condemn, but which had the practical effect of enabling almost every Protestant Nonconformist to follow the dictates of his own conscience without molestation. Scarcely a law in the statute-book is theoretically more objectionable than the Toleration Act. But we question whether in the whole of that vast mass of legislation, from the Great Charter downwards, there be a single law which has so much diminished the sum of human suffering, which has done so much to allay bad passions, which has put an end to so much petty tyranny and vexation, which has brought gladness, peace, and a sense of security to so many private dwellings.

MACAULAY, Essays.

PART II

MODERATELY DIFFICULT

21

There is nothing authors are more apt to lament, than want of encouragement from the age. Whatever their differences in other respects, they are all ready to unite in this complaint, and each indirectly offers himself as an instance of the truth of his assertion.

The beneficed divine, whose wants are only imaginary, expostulates as bitterly as the poorest author. Should interest or good fortune advance the divine to a bishopric, or the poor son of Parnassus into that place which the other has resigned, both are authors no longer : the one goes to prayers once a day, kneels upon cushions of velvet, and thanks gracious Heaven for having made the circumstances of all mankind so extremely happy ; the other battens on all the delicacies of life, enjoys the company of his wife and his easy chair, and sometimes, for the sake of conversation, deplores the luxury of these degenerate days.

All encouragements to merit are therefore misapplied which make the author too rich to continue his profession. There can be nothing more just than the old observation, that authors, like running horses, should be fed, but not fattened. If we would continue them in our service, we should reward them with a little money and a great deal of praise, still keeping their avarice subservient to their ambition. Not that I think a writer incapable of filling an employment with dignity. I would only insinuate, that when made a bishop or statesman he will continue to please us as a writer no longer; as, to resume a former allusion, the running horse, when fattened, will still be fit for very useful purposes, though unqualified for a courser.

No nation gives greater encouragements to learning than we do; yet, at the same time, none are so injudicious in the application. We seem to confer them with the same view that statesmen have been known to grant employments at court, rather as bribes to silence than incentives to emulation.

Upon this principle, all our magnificent endowments of colleges are erroneous; and, at best, more frequently enrich the prudent than reward the ingenious. A lad whose passions are not strong enough in youth to mislead him from that path of science which his tutors, and not his inclinations, have chalked out, by four or five years' perseverance may probably obtain every advantage and honour his college can bestow. I forget whether the simile has been used before, but I would compare the man whose youth has been thus passed in the tranquillity of dispassionate prudence to liquors which never ferment, and, consequently, continue always muddy. Passions may raise a commotion in the youthful breast, but they disturb only to refine it. However this be, mean talents are often rewarded in colleges with an easy subsistence. The candidates for preferments of this kind often regard their admission as a patent for future indolence; so that a life begun in studious labour is often continued in luxurious indolence.

GOLDSMITH, *Inquiry into the Present State of Polite Learning.*

22

I have been sketching an ideal: but one which I seriously recommend to the consideration of all parents; for, though it be impossible and absurd to wish that every young man should grow up a naturalist by profession, yet this age offers no more wholesome training, both moral and intellectual, than that which is given by instilling into the young an early taste for outdoor physical science. The education of our children is now more than ever a puzzling problem, if by education we mean the development of the whole humanity, not merely of some arbitrarily chosen part of it. How to feed the imagination with wholesome food, and teach it to despise French novels, and that sugared slough of sentimental poetry, in comparison with which the old fairy-tales and ballads were manful and rational; how to counteract the tendency to shallowed and conceited sciolism, engendered by hearing popular lectures on all manner of subjects, which can only be really learnt by stern methodic study; how to give habits of enterprise, patience, accurate observation, which the counting-house or the library will never bestow; above all, how to develop the physical powers, without engendering brutality and coarseness,—are questions becoming daily more and more puzzling, while they need daily more and more to be solved in an age of enterprise, travel, and emigration, like the present. For the truth must be told, that the great majority of men who are now distinguished by commercial success, have had a training the directly opposite to that which they are giving to their sons. They are for the most part men who have migrated from the country to the town, and had in their youth the advantages of a sturdy and manful hill-side or sea-side training; men whose bodies were developed, and their lungs fed on pure breezes, long before they brought to work in the city the bodily and mental strength which they gained by loch and moor. But it is not so with their sons. Their business habits are learnt in the counting-house—a good school, doubtless, as far as it goes, but one which will expand none but the lowest intellectual faculties; which will make them accurate accountants, shrewd computers, and competitors, but never the originators of daring schemes, men able and willing to go forth to replenish the earth and subdue it.

KINGSLEY, *Glaucus.*

23

It is the triumph of discipline to overcome both small and great repugnances. We bring ourselves, by its help, to face petty details that are wearisome, and heavy tasks that are almost appalling. Nothing shows the power of discipline more than the application of the mind in the common trades and professions to subjects which have hardly any interest in themselves. Lawyers are especially admirable for this. They acquire the faculty of resolutely applying their minds to the driest documents, with tenacity enough to end in the perfect mastery of their contents—a feat which is utterly beyond the capacity of any undisciplined intellect, however gifted by Nature. In the case of lawyers there are frequent intellectual repugnances to be overcome; but surgeons and other men of science have to vanquish a class of repugnances even less within the power of the will—the instinctive physical repugnances. These are often so strong as to seem apparently insurmountable, but they yield to persevering discipline. Although Haller surpassed his contemporaries in anatomy, and published several important anatomical works, he was troubled at the outset with a horror of dissection beyond what is usual with the inexperienced, and it was only by firm self-discipline that he became an anatomist at all.

There is, however, one reserve to be made about discipline, which is this: we ought not to disregard altogether the mind's preferences and refusals, because in most cases they are the indication of our natural powers. They are not so always; many have felt attracted to the pursuits for which they had no capacity (this happens continually in literature and fine arts), whilst others have greatly distinguished themselves in careers which were not of their own choosing, and for which they felt no vocation in their youth. Still there exists a certain relation between preference and capacity, which may often safely be relied upon, when there are not extrinsic circumstances to attract men or repel them. Discipline becomes an evil, and a very serious evil, causing immense losses of special talent to the community, when it overrides the personal preferences entirely. We are less in danger of this evil, however, from the discipline which we impose upon ourselves than from that which is imposed upon us by the opinion of the society in which we live. The intellectual life has this remarkable peculiarity as to discipline, that whilst very severe discipline is indispensable to it, that which it really needs is the obedience to an inward law, an obedience which is not only compatible with revolt against other people's notions of what the intellectual man ought to think and do, but which often directly leads to such revolt as its own inevitable result   HAMERTON, *The Intellectual Life.*

24

The last resource of the Romans was in the clemency, or at least in the moderation, of the king of the Goths. The senate, who in this emergency assumed the supreme powers of government, appointed two ambassadors to negotiate with the enemy. This important trust was (A.D. 409) delegated to Basilius, a senator, of Spanish extraction, and already conspicuous in the administration of provinces ; and to John, the first tribune of the notaries, who was peculiarly qualified, by his dexterity in business, as well as by his former intimacy with the Gothic prince. When they were introduced into his presence, they declared, perhaps in a more lofty style than became their abject condition, that the Romans were resolved to maintain their dignity, either in peace or war ; and that, if Alaric refused them a fair and honourable capitulation, he might sound his trumpets, and prepare to give battle to an innumerable people, exercised in arms, and animated by despair. "The thicker the hay, the easier it is mowed," was the concise reply of the Barbarian ; and this rustic metaphor was accompanied by a loud and insulting laugh, expressive of his contempt for the menaces of an unwarlike populace, enervated by luxury before they were emaciated by famine. He then condescended to fix the ransom, which he would accept as the price of his retreat from the walls of Rome : *all* the gold and silver in the city, whether it were the property of the state, or of individuals ; *all* the rich and precious moveables ; and *all* the slaves who could prove their title to the name of *Barbarians.* The ministers of the senate presumed to ask, in a modest and suppliant tone, "If such, O King, are your demands, what do you intend to leave us ?" "YOUR LIVES"; replied the haughty conqueror : they trembled, and retired. Yet before they retired, a short suspension of arms was granted, which allowed some time for a more temperate negotiation. The stern features of Alaric were insensibly relaxed ; he abated much of the rigour of his terms ; and at length consented to raise the siege, on the immediate payment of 5000 pounds of gold, of 30,000 pounds of silver, of 4000 robes of silk, of 3000 pieces of fine scarlet cloth, and of 3000 pounds weight of pepper. But the public treasury was exhausted ; the annual rents of the great estates in Italy and the provinces were intercepted by the calamities of war ; the gold and gems had been exchanged, during the famine, for the vilest sustenance ; the hoards of secret wealth were still concealed by the obstinacy of avarice ; and some remains of consecrated spoils afforded the only resource that could avert the impending ruin of the city. As soon as the Romans had satisfied the rapacious demands of Alaric, they were restored, in some measure, to the enjoyment of peace and plenty. Several of the gates were cautiously opened ; the importation of provisions from the river, and the adjacent country, was no longer obstructed by the Goths; the citizens resorted in crowds to the free market, which was held during three days in the suburbs ; and while the merchants who undertook this gainful trade, made a considerable profit, the future subsistence of the city was secured by the ample magazines which were deposited in the public and private granaries.

GIBBON, *Decline and Fall of the Roman Empire.*

25

The meek-eyed Morn appears, mother of dews,
At first faint gleaming in the dappled east,
Till far o'er ether spreads the widening glow;
And from before the lustre of her face
White break the clouds away. With quickened step
Brown Night retires; young Day pours in apace,
And opens all the lawny prospect wide.

The dripping rock, the mountain's misty top
Swell on the sight and brighten with the dawn.
Llue through the dusk the smoking currents shine;
And from the bladed field the fearful hare
Limps awkward: while along the forest glade
The wild deer trip and, often turning, gaze
At early passenger. Music awakes,
The native voice of undissembled joy;
And thick around the woodland hymns arise.
Roused by the cock, the soon-clad shepherd leaves
His mossy cottage, where, with Peace he dwells,
And from the crowded fold in order drives
His flock, to taste the verdure of the morn.
But yonder comes the powerful King of Day
Rejoicing in the east. The lessening cloud,
The kindling azure, and the mountain's brow,
Illumed with fluid gold, his near approach
Betoken glad. Lo! now, apparent all,
Aslant the dew-bright Earth and coloured air,
He looks in boundless majesty abroad,
And sheds the shining day, that burnished plays
On rocks, and hills, and towers, and wandering streams,
High-gleaming from afar.   THOMSON, *The Seasons.*

26

He (Oliver Cromwell) left a fame behind him proportioned to
his extraordinary fortunes and the great qualities which sustained
them ; still more perhaps the admiration of strangers than of his
country, because that sentiment was less alloyed by hatred, which
seeks to extenuate the glory that irritates it. The nation itself
forgave much to one who had brought back the renown of her
ancient story, the tradition of Elizabeth's age, after the ignomin-
ious reigns of her successors. This contrast with James and
Charles in their foreign policy gave additional lustre to the era of

the protectorate. There could not but be a sense of national pride
to see an Englishman, but yesterday raised above the many, without one drop of blood in his veins which the princes of the earth
could challenge as their own, receive the homage of those who
acknowledge no right to power, and hardly any title to respect,
except that of prescription. The sluggish pride of the Court of
Spain, the mean-spirited cunning of Mazarin, the irregular imagination of Christina, sought with emulous ardour the friendship of
our usurper. He had the advantage of reaping the harvest which
he had not sown, by an honourable treaty with Holland, the fruit
of victories achieved under the Parliament. But he still employed
the great energies of Blake in the service for which he was so
eminently fitted; and it is just to say that the maritime glory of
England may first be traced from the era of the Commonwealth
in a track of continuous light. The oppressed Protestants in
Catholic Kingdoms, disgusted at the luke-warmness and half-
apostasy of the Stuarts, looked up to him as their patron and
mediator. Courted by the two rival monarchies of Europe, he
seemed to threaten both with his hostility; and when he declared
against Spain and attacked her West India possessions, with little
pretence certainly of justice, but not by any means, as I conceive,
with the impolicy sometimes charged against him, so auspicious
was his star that the very failure and disappointment of that
expedition obtained a more advantageous possession for England
than all the triumphs of her former Kings.

HALLAM, *Constitutional History.*

27

I consider this mutability of language a wise precaution of
Providence for the benefit of the world at large, and of authors in
particular. To reason from analogy, we daily behold the varied
and beautiful tribes of vegetables springing up, flourishing,
adorning the fields for a short time, and then fading into dust
to make way for their successors. Were not this the case, the

fecundity of nature would be a grievance instead of a blessing. The earth would groan with rank and excessive vegetation, and its surface become a tangled wilderness. In like manner, the works of genius and learning decline, and make way for subsequent productions. Language gradually varies and with it fade away the writings of authors who have flourished their allotted time; otherwise the creative powers of genius would overstock the world and the mind would be completely bewildered in the endless mazes of literature. Formerly there were some restraints on this excessive multiplication. Works had to be transcribed by hand, which was a slow and laborious operation; they were written either on parchment, which was expensive, so that one work was often erased to make way for another; or on papyrus, which was fragile and extremely perishable. Authorship was a limited and unprofitable craft, pursued chiefly by monks in the leisure and solitude of their cloisters. The accumulation of manuscripts was slow and costly, and confined almost entirely to monasteries. To these circumstances it may be owing that we have not been inundated by the intellect of antiquity; that the fountains of thought have not been broken up, and modern genius drowned in the deluge. But the inventions of paper and the press have put an end to all these restraints. They have made everyone a writer, and enabled every mind to pour itself into print, and diffuse itself over the whole intellectual world. The consequences are alarming. The stream of literature has swollen into a torrent, augmented into a river, expanded into a sea. A few centuries since, five or six hundred manuscripts constituted a large library; but what would you say to libraries such as actually exist, containing three or four hundred thousand volumes; legions of authors at the same time busy, and the press going on with fearfully increasing activity to double and quadruple the number? Unless some unforeseen mortality should break out among the progeny of the muse, I tremble for posterity. I fear the mere fluctuation of language will not be sufficient. Criticism may do much. It increases with the increase of literature, and resembles one of those salutary checks on population spoken of by economists.

But let criticism do what it may, writers will write, printers will print, and the world will inevitably be overstocked with good books. It will soon be the employment of a lifetime merely to learn their names. Many a man of passable information at the present day reads scarcely anything but reviews; and before long a man of erudition will be little better than a mere walking catalogue. WASHINGTON IRVING (abridged).

28

But the chief attention both of Charles and of Francis was employed in order to gain the king of England, from whom each of them expected assistance more effectual, and afforded with less political caution. Henry VIII, had ascended the throne of that kingdom in the year one thousand five hundred and nine, with such circumstances of advantage as promised a reign of distinguished felicity and splendour. The union in his person of the two contending titles of York and Lancaster, the alacrity and emulation with which both factions obeyed his commands, not only enabled him to exert a degree of vigour and authority in his domestic government, which none of his predecessors could have safely assumed; but permitted him to take a share in the affairs of the continent, from which the attention of the English had long been diverted by their unhappy intestine divisions. The great sums of money which his father had amassed rendered him the most wealthy prince in Europe. The peace which had subsisted under the cautious administration of that monarch had been of sufficient length to recruit the population of the kingdom after the desolation of the civil wars, but not so long as to enervate its spirit; and the English, ashamed of having rendered their own country so long a scene of discord and bloodshed, were eager to display their valour in some foreign war, and to revive the memory of the victories gained on the continent by their ancestors. Henry's own temper perfectly suited the state of his kingdom, and the disposition of his subjects. Ambitious, active, enterprising, and accomplished in all the martial exercises which in that age formed a chief part of the education of persons of noble birth, and inspired them with an early love of war, he longed to engage in action, and to signalize the beginning of his reign by some remarkable exploit. An opportunity soon presented itself; and the victory at Guinegate, together with the successful sieges of Terouenne and Tournay, though of little utility to England, reflected great lustre on its monarch, and confirmed the idea which foreign princes entertained of his power and consequence. So many concurring causes, added to the happy situation of his own dominions, which secured them from foreign invasion; and to the fortunate circumstance of his being in possession of Calais, which served not only as a key to France, but opened an easy passage into the Netherlands, rendered the king of England the natural guardian of the liberties of Europe, and the arbiter between the emperor and French monarch. Henry himself was sensible of this singular advantage, and convinced that, in order to preserve the balance even, it was his office to prevent either of the rivals from acquiring such superiority of power as might be fatal to the other, or formidable to the rest of Christendom. But he was destitute of the penetration, and still more of the temper, which such a delicate function required. Influenced by caprice, by vanity, by resentment, by affection, he was incapable of forming any regular and extensive system of policy, or of adhering to it with steadiness.

ROBERTSON, *History of the Reign of Charles V.*

29

It happens that I have practically some connexion with schools for different classes of youth ; and I receive many letters from parents respecting the education of their children. In the mass of these letters I am always struck by the precedence which the idea of a " position in life " takes above all other thoughts in the parents'—more especially in the mothers'—minds. "The education befitting such and such a station in life"—this is the phrase, this the object, always. They never seek, as far as I can make out, an education good in itself; even the conception of abstract rightness in training rarely seems reached by the writers. But, an education "which shall keep a good coat on my son's back—which shall enable him to ring with confidence the visitors' bell at double-belled doors; which shall result ultimately in establishment of a double-belled door to his own house—in a word, which shall lead to advancement in life;—*this* we pray for on bent knees—and this is *all* we pray for." It never seems to occur to the parents that there may be an education which, in itself, *is* advancement in Life;—that any other than that may perhaps be advancement in Death; and that this essential education might be more easily got, or given, than they fancy, if they set about it in the right way; while it is for no price, and by no favour, to be got, if they set about it in the wrong.

Indeed, among the ideas most prevalent and effective in the mind of this busiest of countries, I suppose the first—at least that which is confessed with the greatest frankness, and put forward as the fittest stimulus to youthful exertion—is this of "Advancement in Life." May I ask you to consider with me, what this idea practically includes, and what it should include?

Practically, then, at present, "advancement in life" means, becoming conspicuous in life; obtaining a position which shall be acknowledged by others to be respectable or honourable. We do not understand by this advancement, in general, the mere making of money, but the being known to have made it; not the accomplishment of any great aim, but the being seen to have accomplished it. In a word, we mean the gratification of our thirst for applause. That thirst, if the last infirmity of noble minds, is also the first infirmity of weak ones; and, on the whole, the strongest impulsive influence of average humanity: the greatest efforts of the race have always been traceable to the love of praise, as its greatest catastrophes to the love of pleasure.

RUSKIN, Sesame and Lilies.

30

BOADICEA

When the British warrior Queen,
  Bleeding from the Roman rods,
Sought, with an indignant mien,
  Counsel of her country's gods,

Sage beneath a spreading oak
  Sat the Druid, hoary chief;
Every burning word he spoke
  Full of rage, and full of grief:

'Princess! if our aged eyes
  Weep upon thy matchless wrongs,
'Tis because resentment ties
  All the terrors of our tongues.

'Rome shall perish—write that word
  In the blood that she has spilt;
Perish, hopeless and abhorred,
  Deep in ruin as in guilt.

'Rome, for empire far renowned,
  Tramples on a thousand states;
Soon her pride shall kiss the ground—
  Hark! the Gaul is at her gates!

Other Romans shall arise
  Heedless of a soldier's name;
Sounds, not arms, shall win the prize,
  Harmony the path to fame.

'Then the progeny that springs
  From the forests of our land,
Armed with thunder, clad with wings,
  Shall a wider world command.

'Regions Caesar never knew
    Thy posterity shall sway;
Where his eagles never flew,
    None invincible as they.'

Such the bard's prophetic words,
    Pregnant with celestial fire,
Bending as he swept the chords
    Of his sweet but awful lyre.

She, with all a monarch's pride,
    Felt them in her bosom glow ;
Rushed to battle, fought, and died;
    Dying, hurled them at the foe :

'Ruffians, pitiless as proud,
    Heaven awards the vengeance due ;
Empire is on us bestowed,
    Shame and ruin wait for you.'   COWPER.

31

First, the people of the Colonies are descendants of English-
men.   England, Sir, is a nation, which still I hope respects, and
formerly adored her freedom.   The Colonists emigrated from you
when this part of your character was most predominant ; and they
took this bias and direction the moment they parted from your
hands.   They are therefore not only devoted to liberty, but to
liberty according to English ideas, and on English principles.
Abstract liberty, like other mere abstractions, is not to be found.
Liberty inheres in some sensible object, and every nation has
formed to itself some favourite point, which by way of eminence
becomes the criterion of their happiness.   It happened, you know,
Sir, that the great contests for freedom in this country were from
the earliest times chiefly upon the question of taxing.   Most of
the contests in the ancient commonwealths turned primarily on

the right of election of Magistrates; or on the balance among the several orders of the State. The question of money was not with them so immediate. But in England it was otherwise. On this point of taxes, the ablest pens, and most eloquent tongues, have been exercised; the greatest spirits have acted and suffered. In order to give the fullest satisfaction concerning the importance of this point, it was not only necessary for those who in argument defended the excellence of the English constitution, to insist on this privilege of granting money as a dry point of fact, and to prove that the right had been acknowledged in ancient parchments, and blind usages, to reside in a certain body called a House of Commons. They went much further; they attempted to prove and they succeeded, that in theory it ought to be so, from the particular nature of a House of Commons, as an immediate representative of the people; whether the old records had delivered this oracle or not. They took infinite pains to inculcate, as a fundamental principle, that in all Monarchies, the people must in effect themselves, mediately or immediately, possess the power of granting their own money, or no shadow of liberty could subsist. The colonists draw from you, as with their life-blood, these ideas and principles. Their love of liberty, as with you, fixed and attached on this specific point of taxing. Liberty might be safe, or might be endangered, in twenty other particulars, without their being much pleased or alarmed. Here they felt its pulse; and as they found that beat, they thought themselves sick or sound. I do not say whether they were right or wrong in applying your general arguments to their own case. It is not easy indeed to make a monopoly of theorems and corollaries. The fact is, that they did thus apply those general arguments; and your mode of governing them whether through lenity or indolence, through wisdom or mistake, confirmed them in the imagination that they as well as you had an interest in these common principles.

BURKE, *Speech on Conciliation with America.*

32

We should be much mistaken if we pictured to ourselves the squires of the seventeenth century as men bearing a close resemblance to their descendants, the county members and chairmen of quarter sessions with whom we are familiar. The modern country gentleman generally receives a liberal education, passes from a distinguished school to a distinguished college, and has ample opportunity to become an excellent scholar. He has generally seen something of foreign countries. A considerable part of his life has generally been passed in the capital; and the refinements of the capital follow him into the country. There is perhaps no class of dwellings so pleasing as the rural seats of the English gentry. In the parks and pleasure grounds, nature, dressed yet not disguised by art, wears her most alluring form. In the buildings, good sense and good taste combine to produce a happy union of the comfortable and the graceful. The pictures, the musical instruments, the library, would in any other country be considered as proving the owner to be an eminently polished and accomplished man. A country gentleman who witnessed the Revolution was probably in receipt of about a fourth part of the rent which his acres now yield to his posterity. He was, therefore, as compared with his posterity, a poor man, and was generally under the necessity of residing, with little interruption, on his estate. To travel on the Continent, to maintain an establishment in London, or even to visit London frequently, were pleasures in which only the great proprietors could indulge. It may be confidently affirmed that of the squires whose names were then in the Commissions of Peace and Lieutenancy, not one in twenty went to town once in five years, or had ever in his life wandered so far as Paris. Many lords of manors had received an education differing little from that of their menial servants. The heir of an estate often passed his boyhood and youth at the seat of his family with no better tutors than grooms and gamekeepers, and scarce attained learning enough to sign his name to a Mittimus. If he went to school and to college, he generally returned before he was twenty to the seclusion of the old hall, and there, unless his mind were very happily constituted by nature, soon forgot his academical pursuits in rural business and pleasures. MACAULAY, *History of England.*

33

We are at present qualified to view the advantageous position of Constantinople, which appears to have been formed by Nature for the centre and capital of a great monarchy. Situated in the forty-first degree of latitude, the Imperial city commanded, from her seven hills, the opposite shores of Europe and Asia; the climate was healthy and temperate, the soil fertile, the harbour secure and capacious, and the approach on the side of the continent was of small extent and easy defence. The Bosphorus and the Hellespont may be considered as the two gates of Constantinople, and the Prince who possessed those important passages could always shut them against a naval enemy, and open them to the fleets of commerce. The preservation of the eastern provinces may, in some degree, be ascribed to the policy of Constantine, as the barbarians of the Euxine, who in the preceding age had poured their armaments into the heart of the Mediterranean, soon desisted from the exercise of piracy, and despaired of forcing this insurmountable barrier. When the gates of the Hellespont and Bosphorus were shut, the capital still enjoyed within their spacious enclosure every production which could supply the wants, or gratify the luxury of its numerous inhabitants. The sea coasts of Thrace and Bithynia, which languish under the weight of Turkish oppression, still exhibit a rich prospect of vineyards, of gardens, and of plentiful harvests; and the Propontis has ever been renowned for an inexhaustible store of the most exquisite fish, that are taken in their stated seasons, without skill, and almost without labour. But when the passages of the straits were thrown open for trade, they alternately admitted the natural and artificial riches of the north and south, of the Euxine, and of the Mediterranean. Whatever rude commodities were collected in the forests of Germany and Scythia; whatsoever was manufactured by the skill of Europe or Asia; the corn of Egypt, and the gems and spices of the farthest India, were brought by the varying winds into the port of Constantinople, which, for many ages, attracted the commerce of the ancient world.

The prospect of beauty, of safety, and of wealth, united in a single spot, was sufficient to justify the choice of Constantine. But as some decent mixture of prodigy and fable has, in every age, been supposed to reflect a becoming majesty on the origin of great cities, the Emperor was careful to instruct posterity that in obedience to the commands of God he laid the everlasting foundations of Constantinople. On the day consecrated to the foundation of the city, Constantine himself, on foot, with a lance in his hand, led the solemn procession, and directed the line which was traced as the boundary of the destined capital, till the growing circumference was observed with astonishment by the assistants, who, at length, ventured to observe that he had already exceeded the most ample measure of a great city. "I shall still advance," replied Constantine, "till He, the invisible guide who marches before me, thinks proper to stop."

GIBBON, *Decline and Fall of the Roman Empire* (adapted).

34

We cannot enter here into a description of the technical studies for a man of business; but I may point out that there are works which soften the transition from the schools into the world, and which are particularly needed in a system of education, like our own, consisting of studies for the most part remote from real life. These works are such as tend to give the student that interest in the common things about him which he has scarcely ever been called upon to feel. They show how imagination and philosophy can be woven into practical wisdom. Such are the writings of Bacon. His lucid order, his grasp of the subject, the comprehensiveness of his views, his knowledge of mankind—the greatest perhaps that has ever been distinctly given out by any uninspired man—the practical nature of his purposes, and his respect for anything of human interest, render Bacon's works unrivalled in their fitness to form the best men for the conduct of the highest affairs.

It is not, however, so much the thing studied, as the manner of studying it. Our student is not intended to become a learned man, but a man of business; not 'a full man' but 'a ready man.' He must be taught to arrange and express what he knows. For this purpose let him employ himself in making digests, arranging and classifying materials, writing narratives, and in deciding upon conflicting evidence. All these exercises require method. He must expect that his early attempts will be clumsy; he begins, perhaps, by dividing his subject in any way that occurs to him, with no other view than that of treating separate portions of it separately; he does not perceive, at first, what things are of one kind, and what of another, and what should be the logical order of their following. But from such rude beginnings, method is developed; and there is hardly any degree of toil for which he would not be compensated by such a result.

ARTHUR HELPS, *Essays written in the Intervals of Business.*

35

Hardly a chapter of European history or romance is more familiar to the world than the one which records the meteoric course of Charles the Bold. The propriety of his title was never doubtful. No prince was ever bolder, but it is certain that no quality could be less desirable, at that particular moment in the history of his house. It was not the quality to confirm a usurping family in its ill-gotten possessions. Renewed aggressions upon the rights of others justified retaliation and invited attack. Justice, prudence, firmness, wisdom of internal administration were desirable in the son of Philip and the rival of Louis. These attributes the gladiator lacked entirely. His career might have been a brilliant one in the old days of chivalry. His image might have appeared as imposing as the romantic forms of Baldwin Bras de Fer, or Godfrey of Bouillon, had he not been misplaced in history. Nevertheless, he imagined himself governed by a profound policy. He had one dominant idea, to make Burgundy a kingdom. From the moment when, with almost the first standing army known to history, and with coffers well filled by his cautious father's economy, he threw himself into the lists against the crafty Louis, down to the day when he was found dead, naked, deserted, and with his face frozen into a pool of blood and water, he faithfully pursued this thought. His ducal cap was to be exchanged for a kingly crown, while all the provinces which lay beneath the Mediterranean and the North Sea, and between France and Germany, were to be united under his sceptre. The Netherlands, with their wealth, had been already appropriated, and their freedom crushed. Another land of liberty remained ; physically, the reverse of Holland, but stamped with the same courageous nationality, the same ardent love of human rights. Switzerland was to be conquered. Her eternal battlements of ice and granite were to constitute the great bulwark of his realm. The world knows well the result of the struggle between the lord of so many duchies and earldoms, and the Alpine mountaineers. With all his boldness, Charles was but an indifferent soldier. His only merit was physical courage. He imagined himself a consummate commander, and, in conversation with his jester, was fond of comparing himself to Hannibal. "We are getting well Hannibalized to-day, my lord," said the bitter fool, as they rode off together from the disastrous defeat of Gransen. Well "Hannibalized" he was, too, at Gransen, at Murten, and at Nancy. He followed in the track of his prototype only to the base of the mountains.

MOTLEY, *The Rise of the Dutch Republic.*

36

Enter MIRANDA; *and* FERDINAND *bearing a log,*
PROSPERO *behind.*

Miranda.   Alas! now pray you,
Work not so hard: I would the lightning had
Burnt up those logs that you're enjoined to pile!
Pray set it down and rest you: when this burns,
'Twill weep for having wearied you. My father
Is hard at study; pray now rest yourself;
He's safe for these three hours.

Ferdinand.   O most dear mistress,
The sun will set, before I shall discharge
What I must strive to do.

Mira.   If you'll sit down,
I'll bear your logs the while. Pray, give me that;
I'll carry it to the pile.

Ferd.   No, precious creature:
I had rather crack my sinews, break my back,
Than you should such dishonour undergo,
While I sit lazy by.

Mira.   It would become me
As well as it does you: and I should do it
With much more ease; for my good will is to it,
And yours it is against.

Pros. (*Aside*)   Poor worm! thou art infected:
This visitation shows it.

Mira.   You look wearily.

Ferd. No, noble mistress; 'tis fresh morning with me
When you are by at night. I do beseech you—
Chiefly that I might set it in my prayers—
What is your name?

Mira.   Miranda—O my father!
I have broke your hest to say so.

Ferd.   Admir'd Miranda!
Indeed, the top of admiration; worth
What's dearest to the world! Full many a lady
I have ey'd with best regard, and many a time
The harmony of their tongues hath into bondage
Brought my too diligent ear: for several virtues
Have I lik'd several women; never any
With so full soul, but some defect in her
Did quarrel with the noblest grace she ow'd
And put it to the foil: but you, O you!
So perfect and so peerless, are created
Of every creature's best.

Mira.   I do not know
One of my sex; no woman's face remember,
Save from my glass, mine own; nor have I seen
More that I may call men than you, good friend,
And my dear father: how features are abroad,
I am skill-less of; but by my modesty,—
The jewel in my dower,—I would not wish
Any companion in the world but you;
Nor can imagination form a shape
Besides yourself, to like of. But I prattle
Something too wildly and my father's precepts
I therein do forget.

Ferd.   I am in my condition
A prince, Miranda; I do think, a King;—
I would not so!—and would no more endure
This wooden slavery than to suffer
The flesh-fly blow my mouth.—Hear my soul speak:—
The very instant that I saw you, did
My heart fly to your service; there resides
To make me slave to it; and for your sake
Am I this patient log-man.

            SHAKESPERE, *Tempest,* Act III Scene I.

37

In order to throw an odium on political connection, these politicians suppose it a necessary incident to it, that you are blindly to follow the opinions of your party, when in direct opposition to your own clear ideas; a degree of servitude that no worthy man could bear the thought of submitting to; and such as, I believe, no connections, (except some court factions) ever could be so senselessly tyrannical as to impose. Men thinking freely will, in particular instances, think differently. But still, as the greater part of the measures which arise in the course of public business are related, or dependent on, some *great leading principles in government*, a man must be peculiarly unfortunate in the choice of his political company, if he does not agree with them at least nine times in ten. If he does not concur in those general principles upon which the party is founded, and which necessarily draw on a concurrence in their application, he ought from the beginning to have chosen some other, conformable to his opinions. When the question is in its nature doubtful, or not very material, the modesty which becomes an individual, and (in spite of our court moralists) that partiality which becomes a well-chosen friendship, will frequently bring on an acquiescence in the general sentiment. Thus the disagreement will naturally be rare; it will be only enough to indulge freedom, without violating concord, or disturbing arrangement. And this is all that ever was required for a character of the greatest uniformity and steadiness in connection. How men can proceed without any connection at all, is to me utterly incomprehensible; of what sort of materials must that man be made, how must he be tempered and put together, who can sit whole years in Parliament, with five hundred and fifty of his fellow-citizens, amidst the storms of such tempestuous passions, in the sharp conflict of so many wits, and tempers, and characters, in the agitation of such mighty questions, in the discussion of such vast and ponderous interests, without seeing any one sort of men whose character, conduct, or disposition,

would lead him to associate himself with them, to aid and be
aided, in any one system of public utility?

BURKE, *Thoughts on the Cause of the Present Discontents.*

38

The history of England is emphatically the history of progress.
It is the history of a constant movement of the public mind, of a
constant change in the institutions of a great society. We see
that society, at the beginning of the twelfth century, in a state
more miserable than the state in which the most degraded nations
of the East now are. We see it subject to the tyranny of a
handful of armed foreigners. We see a strong distinction of
caste separating the victorious Norman from the vanquished
Saxon. We see the great body of the population in a state of
personal slavery. We see the most debasing and cruel supersti-
tion exercising boundless dominion over the most elevated and
benevolent minds. We see the multitude sunk in brutal ignorance, and the studious few engaged in acquiring what did not
deserve the name of knowledge. In the course of seven centuries
the wretched and degraded race have become the greatest and
most highly civilised people that ever the world saw, have spread
their dominion over every quarter of the globe, have scattered
the seeds of mighty empires and republics over vast continents
of which no dim intimation had ever reached Ptolemy or Strabo,
have created a maritime power which would annihilate in a
quarter of an hour the navies of Tyre, Athens, Carthage, Venice,
and Genoa together, have carried the science of healing, the
means of locomotion and correspondence, every mechanical art,
every manufacture, everything that promotes the convenience of
life, to a perfection which our ancestors would have thought
magical, have produced a literature which may boast of works
not inferior to the noblest which Greece has bequeathed to us,
have discovered the laws which regulate the motions of the
heavenly bodies, have speculated with exquisite subtility on the
operations of the human mind, have been the acknowledged

leaders of the human race in the career of political improvement. The history of England is the history of this great change in the moral, intellectual, and physical state of the inhabitants of our own island. There is much amusing and instructive episodical matter; but this is the main action. To us, we will own, nothing is so interesting and delightful as to contemplate the steps by which the England of Domesday Book, the England of the Curfew and the Forest Laws, the England of crusaders, monks, schoolmen, astrologers, serfs, outlaws, became the England which we know and love, the classic ground of liberty and philosophy, the school of all knowledge, the mart of all trade. The Charter of Henry Beauclerk, the Great Charter, the first assembling of the House of Commons, the extinction of personal slavery, the separation from the See of Rome, the Petition of Right, the Habeas Corpus Act, the Revolution, the establishment of the liberty of unlicensed printing, the abolition of religious disabilities, the reform of the representative system, all these seem to us to be the successive stages of one great revolution; nor can we fully comprehend any one of these memorable events unless we look at it in connection with those which preceded, and with those which followed it. Each of those great and ever-memorable struggles, Saxon against Norman, Villein against Lord, Protestant against Papist, Roundhead against Cavalier, Dissenter against Churchman, Manchester against Old Sarum, was, in its own order and season, a struggle, on the result of which were staked the dearest interests of the human race; and every man who, in the contest which, in his time, divided our country, distinguished himself on the right side is entitled to our gratitude and respect.

MACAULAY, *Essays.*

39

Nature seems to have taken a particular care to disseminate her blessings among the different regions of the world, with an eye to this mutual intercourse and traffic among mankind, that the natives of the several parts of the globe might have a kind of dependence upon one another, and be united together by their common interest. Almost every degree produces something peculiar to it. The food often grows in one country, and the sauce in another. The fruits of Portugal are corrected by the products of Barbadoes, and the infusion of a China plant is sweetened by the pith of an Indian cane. The Philippine Islands give a flavour to our European bowls. The single dress of a woman of quality is often the product of an hundred climates. The muff and the fan come together from the different ends of the earth. The scarf is sent from the torrid zone, and the tippet from beneath the pole. The brocade petticoat rises out of the mines of Peru, and the diamond necklace out of the bowels of Indostan.

If we consider our own country in its natural prospect, without any of the benefits and advantages of commerce, what a barren, uncomfortable spot of earth falls to our share! Natural historians tell us that no fruit grows originally among us, besides hips and haws, acorns and pig-nuts, with other delicacies of the like nature; that our climate of itself, and without the assistance of art, can make no farther advances towards a plum than to a sloe, and carries an apple to no greater perfection than a crab: that our melons, our peaches, our figs, our apricots and cherries, are strangers among us, imported in different ages, and naturalized in our English gardens; and that they would all degenerate and fall away into the trash of our own country, if they were wholly neglected by the planter and left to the mercy of our sun and soil. Nor has traffic more enriched our vegetable world than it has improved the whole face of nature among us. Our ships are laden with the harvest of every climate. Our tables are stored with spices, and oils, and wines. Our rooms are filled with pyramids of China, and adorned with the workmanship of Japan. Our morning draught comes to us from the remotest corners of the earth. We repair our bodies by the drugs of America, and repose ourselves under Indian canopies. My friend, Sir Andrew, calls the vineyards of France our gardens; the spice-islands, our hotbeds; the Persians our silk-weavers, and the Chinese our potters. Nature, indeed, furnishes us with the bare necessaries of life, but traffic gives us a great variety of what is useful, and at the same time supplies us with everything that is convenient and ornamental. Nor is it the least part of this our happiness, that whilst we enjoy the remotest products of the north and south, we are free from those extremities of weather which give them birth ; that our eyes are refreshed with the green fields of Britain, at the same time that our palates are feasted with fruits that rise between the tropics.

For these reasons there are not more useful members in a commonwealth than Merchants. They knit mankind together in a mutual intercourse of good offices, distribute the gifts of Nature, find work for the poor, add wealth to the rich, and magnificence to the great. Our English merchant converts the tin of his own country into gold, and exchanges its wool for rubies. The Mahommedans are clothed in our British manufacture, and the inhabitants of the frozen zone warmed with the fleeces of our sheep.   ADDISON, *The Spectator.*

40

It was to this turmoil of men's minds, this wayward luxuriance and prodigality of fancy, that we owe the revival of English letters under Elizabeth. Here, as elsewhere, the Renascence found vernacular literature all but dead, poetry reduced to the doggrel of Skelton, history to the annals of Fabyan or Halle. It had however done little for English letters. The overpowering influence of the new models both of thought and style which it gave to the world in the writers of Greece and Rome was at first felt only as a fresh check to the dreams of any revival of English poetry or prose. Though England shared more than any European country in the political and ecclesiastical results of the New Learning, its literary results were far less than in the rest of Europe, in Italy, or Germany, or France. More alone ranks among the great classical scholars of the sixteenth century. Classical learning indeed all but perished at the Universities in the storm of the Reformation, nor did it revive there till the close of Elizabeth's reign. Insensibly however the influences of the Renascence fertilized the intellectual soil of England for the rich harvest that was to come. The court poetry which clustered round Wyatt and Surrey, exotic and imitative as it was, promised a new life for English verse. The growth of Grammar Schools realized the dream of Sir Thomas More, and brought the middle-classes, from the squire to the petty tradesman, into contact with the masters of Greece and Rome. The love of travel, which became so remarkable a characteristic of Elizabeth's day, quickened the intelligence of the wealthier nobles. "Home-keeping youths," says Shakespeare in words that mark the time, "have ever homely wits," and a tour over the Continent was just becoming part of the education of a gentleman. Fairfax's version of Tasso, Harrington's version of Ariosto, were signs of the influence which the literature of Italy, the land to which travel led most frequently, exerted on English minds. The writers of Greece and Rome began at last to tell upon England when they were popularized by a crowd of translations. Chapman's noble version of Homer stands high above its fellows, but all the greater poets and historians of the classical world were turned into English before the close of the sixteenth century. It is characteristic of England that historical literature was the first to rise from its long death, though the form in which it rose marked the difference between the world in which it had perished, and that in which it reappeared. During the Middle Ages the world had been without a past, save the shadowy and unknown past of early Rome; and annalist and chronicler told the story of the years which went before, as a preface to his tale of the present without a sense of any difference between them.

GREEN, *A Short History of the English People.*

PART III

DIFFICULT

41

While improvements so important with respect to the state of society and the administration of justice gradually made progress in Europe, sentiments more liberal and generous had begun to animate the nobles. These were inspired by the spirit of chivalry, which, though considered commonly as a wild institution, the effect of caprice and the source of extravagance, arose naturally from the state of society at that period, and had a very serious influence in refining the manners of the European nations. The feudal state was a state of almost perpetual war, rapine, and anarchy, during which the weak and unarmed were exposed to insults or injuries. The most effectual protection against violence and oppression was often found to be that which the valour and generosity of private persons afforded. The same spirit of enterprise which had prompted so many gentlemen to take arms in defence of the oppressed pilgrims in Palestine, incited others to declare themselves the patrons and avengers of injured innocence at home. When the final reduction of the Holy Land under the dominion of infidels put an end to these foreign expeditions, the latter was the only employment left for the activity and courage of adventurers. To check the insolence of overgrown oppressors, to rescue the helpless from captivity; to protect or to avenge women, orphans, and ecclesiastics, who could not bear arms in their own defence; to redress wrongs, and to remove grievances, were deemed acts of the highest prowess and merit. Valour, humanity, courtesy, justice, honour, were the characteristic qualities of chivalry. To these was added religion, which mingled itself with every passion and institution during the middle ages, and, by infusing a large proportion of enthusiastic zeal, gave them such force as carried them to romantic excess. This singular institution, in which valour, gallantry, and religion were so strangely blended, was wonderfully adapted to the taste and genius of martial nobles; and its effects were soon visible in their manners. War was carried on with less ferocity, when humanity came to be deemed the ornament of knighthood no less than courage. More gentle and polished manners were introduced, when courtesy was recommended as the most amiable of knightly virtues. A scrupulous adherence to truth, with the most religious attention to fulfil every engagement, became the distinguishing characteristic of a gentleman, because chivalry was regarded as the school of honour, and inculcated the most delicate sensibility with respect to those points. The admiration of these qualities, together with the high distinctions and prerogatives conferred on knighthood in every part of Europe, inspired persons of noble birth on some occasions with a species of military fanaticism and led them to extravagant enterprises. But they deeply imprinted on their minds the principles of generosity and honour. These were strengthened by everything that can affect the senses, or touch the heart. Perhaps the humanity which accompanies all the operations of war, the refinements of gallantry, and the point of honour, the three chief circumstances which distinguish modern from ancient manners, may be ascribed in a great measure to this institution, which has appeared whimsical to superficial observers, but by its effects has proved of great benefit to mankind. The sentiments which chivalry inspired, had a wonderful influence on manners and conduct during the twelfth, thirteenth, and fourteenth centuries. They were so deeply rooted, that they continued to operate after the vigour and reputation of the institution itself began to decline.

ROBERTSON, *History of the Reign of Charles V.* (abridged).

42

But feelings more suitable to the purpose of their visit to Martindale Castle were awakened in the bosoms even of these stern sectaries, when the lady of the Castle, still in the very prime of beauty and of womanhood, appeared at the top of the breach with her principal female attendants, to receive her guests with the honour and courtesy becoming her invitation. She had laid aside the black dress which had been her sole attire for several years, and was arrayed with a splendour not unbecoming her high descent and quality. Jewels, indeed, she had none ; but her long and dark hair was surmounted with a chaplet made of oak leaves, interspersed with lilies ; the former being the emblem of the king's preservation in the Royal Oak, and the latter, of his happy Restoration. What rendered her presence still more interesting to those who looked on her, was the presence of the two children whom she held in either hand ; one of whom was well known to them all to be the child of their leader, Major Bridgenorth, who had been restored to life and health by the almost maternal care of Lady Peveril.

If even the inferior persons of the party felt the healing influence of her presence, thus accompanied, poor Bridgenorth was almost overwhelmed with it. The strictness of his caste and manners permitted him not to sink on his knee and kiss the hand which held his little orphan ; but the deepness of his obeisance—the faltering tremor of his voice—and the glistening of his eye, showed a grateful respect for the lady whom he addressed—deeper and more reverential than could have been expressed even by Persian prostration. A few courteous and mild words, expressive of the pleasure she found in once more seeing her neighbours as her friends—a few kind inquiries, addressed to the principal individuals among her guests, concerning their families and connections, completed her triumph over angry thoughts and dangerous recollections, and disposed men's bosoms to sympathise with the purposes of the meeting.

Even Solsgrace himself, although imagining himself bound by
his office and duty to watch over and counteract the wiles of the
"Amalekitish woman," did not escape the sympathetic infection ;
being so much struck with the marks of peace and good-will
exhibited by Lady Peveril, that he immediately raised the psalm—

> "O what a happy thing it is,
> And joyful for to see,
> Brethren to dwell together in
> Friendship and unity!"

Accepting this salutation as a mark of courtesy repaid, the
Lady Peveril marshalled in person this party of her guests to the
apartment, where ample good cheer was provided for them ; and
had even the patience to remain while Master Nehemiah Solsgrace
pronounced a benediction of portentous length, as an introduction
to the banquet. Her presence was in some measure a restraint
on the worthy divine, whose prolusion lasted the longer, and was
the more intricate and embarrassed, that he felt himself debarred
from rounding it off by his usual alliterative petition for deliver-
ance from Popery, Prelacy, and Peveril of the Peak, which had
become so habitual to him, that, after various attempts to conclude
with some other form of words, he found himself at last obliged
to pronounce the first words of his usual formula aloud, and
mutter the rest in such a manner as not to be intelligible even by
those who stood nearest to him.

The minister's silence was followed by all the various sounds
which announce the onset of a hungry company on a well-
furnished table ; and at the same time gave the lady an opportunity to leave the apartment, and look to the accommodation
of her other company. She felt, indeed, that it was high time to
do so ; and that the Royalist guests might be disposed to
misapprehend, or even to resent, the prior attentions which she
had thought it prudent to offer to the Puritans.

These apprehensions were not altogether ill-founded. It was
in vain that the steward had displayed the royal standard, with
its proud motto of "Tandem Triumphans," on one of the great

towers which flanked the main entrance of the Castle; while from the other floated the banner of Peveril of the Peak, under which many of those who now approached had fought during all the vicissitudes of civil war. It was in vain he repeated his clamorous "Welcome, noble Cavaliers! welcome, generous gentlemen!" There was a slight murmur amongst them, that their welcome ought to have come from the mouth of the Colonel's lady—not from that of a menial. Sir Jasper Cranbourne, who had sense as well as spirit and courage, and who was aware of his fair cousin's motives, having been indeed consulted by her upon all the arrangements which she had adopted, saw matters were in such a state that no time ought to be lost in conducting the guests to the banqueting apartment, where a fortunate diversion from all these topics of rising discontent might be made, at the expense of the good cheer of all sorts, which the lady's care had so liberally provided.

The stratagem of the old soldier succeeded in its utmost extent. He assumed the great oaken chair occupied by the steward at his audits; and Doctor Dummerar having pronounced a brief Latin benediction (which was not the less esteemed by the hearers that none of them understood it), Sir Jasper exhorted the company to whet their appetites to the dinner by a brimming cup to his Majesty's health, filled as high and as deep as their goblets would permit. In a moment all was bustle, with the clang of wine-cups and of flagons. In another moment the guests were on their feet like so many statues, all hushed as death, but with eyes glancing with expectation, and hands out-stretched, which displayed their loyal brimmers. The voice of Sir Jasper, clear, sonorous, and emphatic, as the sound of his war-trumpet, announced the health of the restored monarch, hastily echoed back by the assemblage, impatient to render it due homage. Another brief pause was filled by the draining of their cups, and the mustering breath to join in a shout so loud, that not only the rafters of the old hall trembled while they echoed it back, but the garlands of oaken boughs and flowers with which they were decorated, waved wildly, and rustled as if agitated by a sudden whirlwind. This rite observed, the company proceeded to assail the good cheer with which the table groaned, animated as they were to the attack both by mirth and melody, for they were attended by all the minstrels of the district, who, like the Episcopal clergy, had been put to silence during the reign of the self-entitled saints of the Commonwealth. The social occupation of good eating and drinking, the exchange of pledges betwixt old neighbours who had been fellow-soldiers in the moment of resistance—fellow-sufferers in the time of depression and subjugation, and were now partners in the same general subject of congratulation, soon wiped from their memory the trifling cause of complaint which in the minds of some had darkened the festivity of the day; so that, when the Lady Peveril walked into the hall, accompanied as before with the children and her female attendants, she was welcomed with the acclamations due to the mistress of the banquet and of the Castle—the dame of the noble knight who had led most of them to battle with an undaunted and persevering valour, which was worthy of better success.

Her address to them was brief and matronly, yet spoken with so much feeling as found its way to every bosom. She apologized for the lateness of her personal welcome, by reminding them that there were then present in Martindale Castle that day, persons whom recent happy events had converted from enemies into friends, but on whom the latter character was so recently imposed, that she dared not neglect with them any point of ceremonial. But those whom she now addressed were the best, the dearest, the most faithful friends of her husband's house, to whom and to their valour Peveril had not only owed those successes, which had given them and him fame during the late unhappy times, but to whose courage she in particular had owed the preservation of their leader's life, even when it could not avert defeat. A word or two of heartfelt congratulation on the happy restoration of the royal line and authority, completed all which she had boldness to add, and, bowing gracefully round her, she lifted a cup to her lips as if to welcome her guests.

There still remained, and especially amongst the old Cavaliers of the period, some glimmering of that spirit which inspired Froissart, when he declares that a knight hath double courage at need, when animated by the looks and words of a beautiful and virtuous woman. It was not until the reign which was commencing at the moment we are treating of, that the unbounded licence of the age, introducing a general course of profligacy, degraded the female sex into mere servants of pleasure, and, in so doing, deprived society of that noble tone of feeling towards the sex, which, considered as a spur to "raise the clear spirit," is superior to every other impulse, save those of religion and of patriotism. The beams of the ancient hall of Martindale Castle instantly rang with a shout louder and shriller than that at which they had so lately trembled, and the names of the Knight of the Peak and his lady were proclaimed amid waving of caps and hats, and universal wishes for their health and happiness.

SCOTT, *Peveril of the Peak.*

43

To the Earl of Chesterfield,

February 7, 1755.

MY LORD,

I have been lately informed by the proprietor of "The World" that two papers in which my Dictionary is recommended to the public were written by your Lordship. To be so distinguished is an honour, which, being very little accustomed to favours from the great, I know not well how to receive, or in what terms to acknowledge.

When, upon some slight encouragement, I first visited your Lordship, I was overpowered, like the rest of mankind, by the enchantment of your address, and could not forbear to wish that I might boast myself "Le vainqueur du vainqueur de la terre"; that I might obtain that regard for which I saw the world contending; but I found my attendance so little encouraged, that neither pride nor modesty would suffer me to continue it. When I had once addressed your Lordship in public, I had exhausted all the art of pleasing which a retired and uncourtly scholar can possess. I had done all that I could; and no man is well pleased to have his all neglected, be it ever so little.

Seven years, my lord, have now passed, since I waited in your outward rooms, or was repulsed from your door; during which time I have been pushing on my work through difficulties, of which it is useless to complain, and have brought it, at last, to the verge of publication, without one act of assistance, one word of encouragement, or one smile of favour. Such treatment I did not expect, for I never had a patron before.

The shepherd in Vergil grew at last acquainted with Love, and found him a native of the rocks.

Is not a patron, my lord, one who looks with unconcern on a man struggling for life in the water, and when he has reached ground, encumbers him with help? The notice which you have been pleased to take of my labours, had it been early, had been kind; but it has been delayed till I am indifferent, and cannot enjoy it; till I am solitary, and cannot impart it; till I am known, and do not want it. I hope it is no very cynical asperity not to confess obligations where no benefit has been received, or to be unwilling that the public should consider me as owing that to a patron, which Providence has enabled me to do for myself.

Having carried on my work thus far with so little obligation to any favourer of learning, I shall not be disappointed though I should conclude it, if less be possible, with less; for I have been long wakened from that dream of hope in which I once boasted myself with so much exultation,

My lord,

Your lordship's most humble,

most obedient servant,

SAM. JOHNSON.

BOSWELL, *Life of Johnson.*

44

A curious, and as we think, not inapt parallel, might be drawn between Mr. Lincoln and one of the most striking figures in modern history—Henry IV. of France. The career of the latter may be more picturesque, as that of a daring captain always is; but in all its vicissitudes there is nothing more romantic than that sudden change, as by a rub of Aladdin's Lamp, from the attorney's office in a country town of Illinois to the helm of a great nation in times like these. The analogy between the characters and circumstances of the two men is in many respects singularly close. Succeeding to a rebellion rather than a crown, Henry's chief material dependence was the Huguenot party, whose doctrines sat upon him with a looseness distasteful certainly, if not suspicious, to the more fanatical among them. King only in name over the greater part of France, and with his capital barred against him, it yet gradually became clear to the more far-seeing even of the Catholic party, that he was the only centre of order and legitimate authority round which France could re-organise itself. While preachers who held the divine right of kings made the churches of Paris ring with declamations in favour of democracy rather than submit to the heretic dog of a Béarnois—much as our *soi-disant* Democrats have lately been preaching the divine right of slavery, and denouncing the heresies of the Declaration of Independence—Henry bore both parties in hand till he was convinced that only one course of action could possibly combine his own interests and those of France. Meanwhile the Protestants believed somewhat doubtfully that he would be theirs, and Henry himself turned aside remonstrance, advice, and curiosity alike with a jest or a proverb (if a little *high*, he liked them none the worse), joking continually as his manner was.

We have seen Mr. Lincoln contemptuously compared to Sancho Panza by persons incapable of appreciating one of the deepest pieces of wisdom in the profoundest romance ever written; namely, that, while Don Quixote was incomparable in theoretic and ideal statesmanship, Sancho, with his stock of proverbs, the ready money of human experience, made the best possible practical governor. Henry IV. was as full of wise saws and modern instances as Mr. Lincoln, but beneath all this was the thoughtful, practical, humane, and thoroughly earnest man, around whom the fragments of France were to gather themselves till she took her place again as a planet of the first magnitude in the European system. In one respect Mr. Lincoln was more fortunate than Henry. However some may think him wanting in zeal, the most fanatical can find no taint of apostasy in any measure of his, nor can the most bitter charge him with being influenced by motives of personal interest. The leading distinction between the policies of the two is one of circumstances. Henry went over to the nation; Mr. Lincoln has steadily drawn the nation over to him. One left a united France; the other, we hope and believe, will leave a re-united America. We leave our readers to trace the further points of difference and resemblance for themselves, merely suggesting a general similarity which has often occurred to us.

J. R. LOWELL, *My Study Windows.*

45

In looking back to the great works of genius in former times, we are sometimes disposed to wonder at the little progress which has since been made in poetry, and in the arts of imitation in general. But this is perhaps a foolish wonder. Nothing can be more contrary to the fact, than the supposition that in what we understand by the *fine arts*, as painting, and poetry, relative perfection is only the result of repeated efforts in successive periods, and that what has been once well done, constantly leads to something better. What is mechanical, reducible to rule, or capable of demonstration, is progressive, and admits of gradual improvement: what is not mechanical, or definite, but depends upon feeling, taste, and genius, very soon becomes stationary, or retrograde, and loses more than it gains by transfusion. The contrary opinion is a vulgar error, which has grown up, like many others, from transferring an analogy of one kind to something quite distinct, without taking into the account the difference in the nature of the things, or attending to the difference of the results. For most persons, finding what wonderful advances have been made in biblical criticism, in chemistry, in mechanics, in geometry, astronomy, etc.; *i.e.* in things depending on mere inquiry and experiment, or on absolute demonstration, have been led hastily to conclude that there was a general tendency in the efforts of the human intellect to improve by repetition, and, in all other arts and institutions, to grow perfect and mature by time. We look back upon the theological creed of our ancestors, and their discoveries in natural philosophy, with a smile of pity: science, and the arts connected with it, have all had their infancy, their youth, and manhood, and seem to contain in them no principle of limitation or decay: and, enquiring no farther about the matter, we infer, in the intoxication of our pride, and the height of our self-congratulation, that the same progress has been made, and will continue to be made, in all other things which are the work of man. The fact, however, stares us so plainly in the face that one would think the smallest reflection must suggest the truth, and overturn our sanguine theories. The greatest poets, the ablest orators, the best painters, and the finest sculptors that the world ever saw, appeared soon after the birth of these arts, and lived in a state of society which was, in other respects, comparatively barbarous. Those arts, which depend on individual genius and incommunicable power, have always leaped at once from infancy to manhood, from the first rude dawn of invention to their meridian height and dazzling lustre, and have in general declined ever after. This is the peculiar distinction and privilege of each, of science, and of art:—of the one, never to attain its utmost limit of perfection; and of the other, to arrive at it almost at once. **W. Hazlitt,** *Lectures on the English Poets.*

46

Observe the accommodation of the most common artificer or day-labourer in a civilised and thriving country, and you will perceive that the number of people of whose industry a part, though but a small part, has been employed in procuring him this accommodation exceeds all computation. The woollen coat, for example, which covers the day-labourer, as coarse and rough as it may appear, is the produce of the joint labour of a great multitude of workmen. The shepherd, the sorter of the wool, the wool-comber or carder, the dyer, the scribbler, the spinner, the weaver, the fuller, the dresser, with many others, must all join their different arts in order to complete even this homely production. How many merchants and carriers, besides, must have been employed in transporting the materials from some of those work-men to others who often live in a very distant part of the country! How much commerce and navigation in particular, how many ship-builders, sailors, sail-makers, rope-makers, must have been employed in order to bring together the different drugs made use of by the dyer, which often come from the remotest corners of the world! What a variety of labour, too, is necessary in order to produce the tools of the meanest of these workmen! To say nothing of such complicated machines as the ship of the sailor, the mill of the fuller, or even the loom of the weaver, let us consider only what a variety of labour is requisite in order to form that very simple machine, the shears with which the shepherd clips the wool. The miner, the builder of the furnace for smelting the ore, the feller of the timber, the burner of the charcoal to be made use in the smelting house, the brick-maker, the brick-layer, the workmen who attend the furnace, the mill-wright, the forger, the smith, must all of them join their different arts in order to produce them.

Were we to examine in the same manner all the different parts of his dress and household furniture, the coarse linen shirt which he wears next his skin, the shoes which cover his feet, the bed which he lies on, and all the different parts which compose it, the kitchen grate at which he prepares his victuals, the coals which he makes use of for that purpose, dug from the bowels of the earth, and brought to him perhaps by a long sea and a long land carriage, all the other utensils of his kitchen, all the furniture of his table, the knives and forks, the earthen or pewter plates upon which he serves up and divides his victuals, the different hands employed in preparing his bread and his beer, the glass window which lets in the heat and the light, and keeps out the wind and the rain, with all the knowledge and art requisite for preparing that beautiful and happy invention, without which these northern parts of the world could scarce have afforded a very comfortable habitation, together with the tools of all the different workmen employed in producing these different conveniences; if we examine, I say, all these things, and consider what a variety of labour is employed about each of them, we shall be sensible that without the assistance and co-operation of many thousands, the very meanest person in a civilised country could not be provided, even according to what we very falsely imagine, the easy and simple manner in which he is commonly accommodated. Compared, indeed, with the more extravagant luxury of the great, his accommodation must no doubt appear extremely simple and easy; and yet it may be true, perhaps, that the accommodation of an European prince does not always so much exceed that of an industrious and frugal peasant, as the accommodation of the latter exceeds that of many an African king, the absolute master of the lives and liberties of ten thousand naked savages.

ADAM SMITH, *Wealth of Nations.*

47

THE CONGO QUESTION—GROWTH OF PUBLIC OPINION.

BRUSSELS, *May 7th.*

Now that the first stage of the debate is over, it may be interesting to note the present position of affairs. The debate itself has been conducted throughout in a manner worthy of its subject. The discussion has been serious, and, for the most part, to the point, though few speakers have been able altogether to forget those party considerations which, ever prominent in this country, bulk even larger as the elections draw near.

The Government has shown much prudence, from its own point of view, in putting no obstacle in the way of free discussion. If it had persisted in its original alleged intention of forcing a vote before the elections, it would have enabled its opponents to go to the country with the cry that the voice of the people was being stifled. Now, not only has that cry been neutralized, but the course of the debate has emphasized the differences which exist in the Liberal party on this particular question, so that they will have to fall back on the programme on which alone they are united. On the other hand, it is possible that the obstructive tactics which would inevitably have been adopted by the Opposition, if their views had not been met, would have damaged them in the eyes of the country, and to that extent have benefited the Government; but the price would have been a casting to the winds of the decencies of debate. One interesting feature of the debate has been the frank recognition of the outrageous character of the Congo regime, and the determination expressed by annexationists to institute immediate reforms. The "English campaign," supported as it has been by the report of the Belgian Commission of Inquiry and other trustworthy documents, is now admitted to have been justified. Belgian politicians are now fully alive to their future responsibilities in the matter of reforms, and there seems no reason why the measured steps of diplomacy should not lead to a definite understanding which will satisfy all reasonable requirements.

Another interesting feature has been the equally frank recognition of the identity of the Sovereign of the Congo and the King of the Belgians. This is an extremely awkward and painful subject for Royalists, and nothing shall be said to emphasize it here, except to point out that it has been a severe strain even upon the most loyal Belgians to attribute all the honour and glory of the discovery and development of the Congo to the

King, while repudiating the objectionable characteristics of the process as the acts of the Sovereign of an entirely independent State. But one point which could not fail to impress an observer of the debate has been the way in which the most full-blooded condemnation of the King has passed without protest, no doubt from the consciousness that his Majesty's proceedings of late years, both at home and abroad, are impossible for the most abandoned casuist to justify.

The Congo question is the Belgian "affaire Dreyfus." Among intelligent men it has produced similar differences of opinion and similar searchings of heart. It is being abundantly discussed among the mass of the people, hitherto indifferent to it. The result will be good for Belgium, quite apart from whether the Colony is or is not all that it is hoped or feared to be, if it leads the country to take a wider and more serious view of its destiny, and if it in any way removes the impression, so diligently fostered by the Congo Press Bureau, that England's motives in the matter have been as "interested" as the campaign against her has been ill-informed or corrupt.

Central Welsh Board, July 1908.

48

And now the time in special is, by privilege to write and speak what may help to the further discussing of matters in agitation. The temple of *Janus* with his two *controversal* faces might now not unsignificantly be set open. And though all the winds of doctrine were let loose to play upon the earth, so Truth be in the field, we do injuriously by licensing and prohibiting to misdoubt her strength. Let her and Falsehood grapple; who ever knew Truth put to the worse, in a free and open encounter? Her confuting is the best and surest suppressing. He who hears what praying there is for light and clearer knowledge to be sent down among us, would think of other matter to be constituted beyond the discipline of *Geneva*, framed and fabricked already to our hands. Yet when the new light which we beg for shines in upon us, there be who envy, and oppose, if it come not first in at their casements. What a collusion is this, whenas we are exhorted by the wise man to use diligence, *to seek for wisdom as for hidden treasures* early and late, that another order shall enjoin us to know nothing but by statute! When a man hath been labouring the hardest labour in the deep mines of knowledge, hath furnished out his findings in all their equipage, drawn forth his reasons as it were a battle ranged, scattered and defeated all objections in his way, calls out his adversary into the plain, offers him the advantage of wind and sun, if he please, only that he may try the matter by dint of argument, for his opponents then to skulk, to lay ambushments, to keep a narrow bridge of licensing where the challenger should pass, though it be valour enough in soldiership, is but weakness and cowardice in the wars of Truth. For who knows not that Truth is strong, next to the Almighty? She needs no policies, no stratagems, nor licensings to make her victorious; those are the shifts and the defences that error uses against her power. Give her but room, and do not bind her when she sleeps, for then she speaks not true, as the old *Proteus* did, who spake oracles only when he was caught and bound, but then rather she turns herself into all shapes, except her own, and perhaps tunes her voice according to the time, as Micaiah did before Ahab, until she be adjured into her own likeness.

MILTON, *Areopagitica.*

49

(This exercise should be turned into indirect speech.)

I would now ask you to look at Scott as a writer of prose fiction, who, from the stores of his learning and the spring of his imagination, fed for sixteen years the fancy of the civilised world, ministering no less to the social and moral well-being than to the innocent gaiety of nations. The Waverley Novels provided a new pleasure for the reading world, even for the little fastidious world of jaded elderly critics. To him who has never seen the sea or the mountains, the first sight of either becomes an epoch in his life. Many of us, I believe, cherish as a choice reminiscence our first glimpse of the fair imaginary realm which was created by Scott. My own first peep of it I well remember, obtained by means of a review which I got hold of when at an age at which the nature and uses of quarterly criticism were for me as yet very dim. The delight with which I devoured the extracts in small print was only equalled by the disgust with which I floundered amongst the comments in a larger type, lamentable fits of insanity, as I thought them, befalling in some mysterious manner my matchless story-teller. It was not till several years afterwards that the book itself fell into my hands, and the well-remembered names of Isaac of York, Rebecca, and Rowena, told me that I had found an old friend in *Ivanhoe.* I venture to mention this trivial personal incident in hopes that it may recall to many of you whom I have the honour to address, various green spots, diverse and yet similar, of auld lang syne connected with Scott and his writings. (Applause.) The effect which the first Waverley Novel may produce on a fresh and imaginative mind, now when Scott has taught his craft to so many cunning hands, can give but a very faint idea of the success of *Waverley.* The "small anonymous sort of a novel," as Scott called it in sending it to Mr. Morritt by the mail of the 9th July, 1814, very speedily took the world by storm. Five years later, on the publication of the eighth of the series, a reviewer so discriminating and so little given to reckless praise announced that no such prodigy had been known since Shakspeare wrote his thirty-eight plays in the brief space of his early manhood. This opinion was recorded upon the appearance of *Kenilworth*, *Nigel*, *Durward*, and various other favourites, scarce less successful than their predecessors. Detailed criticism would be out of place here, where we are met to agree that as Stratford did for Shakspeare, so Edinburgh must do for Scott. The long procession of ideal figures, headed by Waverley and the Baron of Bradwardine, and closed by Richard Middlemas and the French Begum, forms stern and solemn, or gay and sportive, correct or grotesque, of every age and sex, of many

desires, periods, and modes of mind, which proceeded from the
brain of Scott, have furnished a goodly quota of their number to
the world's gallery, where the people of the poet's dream stand
side by side with the personages of history, and where it often
occurs to us, who are the transitory visitors to the show, to
exclaim with the Spanish monk before the canvas of Titian —

> "These are the real men,
> And we the painted shadows on the wall."

(Applause.) Who of us, indeed, do not feel Don Quixote and
his squire, Hamlet and Falstaff, to be our fellow-creatures quite
as truly as Philip III. or the Minister Lerma, or Devereux, Cecil,
or Queen Bess herself? Scott has filled more places in the
historical Valhalla than any other writer, Shakspeare alone
excepted. To the history of this little corner of Northern Europe,
this single Scotchman, bending his big brow over his desk, has
given a wide and splendid celebrity, far beyond the reach, at
least far beyond the attainment of the strong hands and stout
hearts and busy brains of the whole perfervid race of other days
at home and abroad. (Applause.) His reading of our national
story is probably the version which will long be accepted by the
world. In one point, indeed, it was fiercely challenged. The
sufferings and services of the Covenanters had made them popular
idols, and some good men were startled at being shown that their
idols had a comic side, and on being reminded that in respect
and sympathy for freedom of thought the black Prelatist and the
true-blue Presbyterian were in the relative condition of the pot
and the kettle in the fable. But I question if any of the contro-
versialists who entered the field against Scott ever recognized
more fully than he did that the spirit which leads men to lay
down their lives for what they hold to be truth is the very breath
of national life; if any Whig writer has ever painted a more
touching picture of the bitter men of Bothwellhaugh than the
novelist who delighted to wear the white cockade of the cavalier.
In fact, the good corn of the history of the Kirk seems to owe
quite as much to the winnowing it received from Scott as to the

painful garnerings of honest Wodrow, in whose husbandry flail and fanner were unknown. If the world beyond the Tweed is likely for long to read Scottish history with the eyes of Scott, it is still more certain to adopt his estimate of the character of our people. Coleridge used to say, " Whenever I have occasion to speak of a Scotch rascal, I always lay the emphasis on Scotch." This principle Scott applied in a somewhat larger spirit. His Scotch characters, Highland and Lowland, tinted with all the delicate shades of local and social colour, gentle and simple, good and bad, are all emphatically Scotch. It is not for a Scotchman to say whether our great painter has or has not been

> " To all our virtues very kind,
> To all our faults a little blind."

But we certainly ought to be well content with the national portraiture, and do each what in us lies to perpetuate its nobler features. The work that Burns yearned after from the depths of his passionate heart, Scott has actually accomplished. From the story of our feuds and factions, from the dust and blood of the past, his genius and his patriotism have culled all that was pure and lovely and of good report, and have woven it into an immortal chaplet for the brow of Caledonia. He has fanned the fire of Scottish nationality without detriment—nay, with positive advantage to that higher and nobler nationality which rallies around the flag whereon the white cross fits so compactly into the red. Wherever the British flag flies, it will find no better or truer defenders there than those Scotchmen who best know and love their Scott. (Applause.)

Amidst moral and intellectual benefits, I must not forget the important contributions of Scott to the material prosperity of his native land. The dead poet whom we celebrate is as distinctly an employer of labour as any of those captains of industry whose looms whirl by the Tweed, or whose furnaces flame along the Clyde. Here, there, everywhere, pilgrims are flocking to the shrines which he has built for himself and his country ; and trades and occupations of all kinds flourish by the brain which lies in

Dryburgh, as they formerly flourished by the brain of St. Thomas. Mrs Dodds of the Cleikum, Neil Blane of the Howff, and others, his pleasant publicans, are only a few of those whom Scott has established in a roaring business. When land is to be sold in any district of the Scott countries, his scenes and his characters therewith connected, and even his passing allusions, are carefully chronicled amongst other attractions in the advertisement, and duly inventoried amongst the title-deeds of the estate. It would be hard to say how many years' purchase Scott has added to the value of Branksome, or of the Eildon pastures. But there is no doubt that the touch of his pen does in many places form an important element of that unearned increment of value—that, I believe, is the scientific term—which Mr. Stuart Mill and friends propose shortly to transfer from the lords of the soil to the Lords of the Treasury. Some of Scott's truest admirers have been disposed to regret that there is no single piece of his that gives any adequate idea of his greatness. The pangs of parturition were indeed unknown to that most prolific of brains. The mighty machinery of his mind worked with the least possible friction. *Waverley* is generally esteemed the most carefully finished of his tales, yet we know, on his own authority, the two last volumes were written between the 4th of June and the 1st of July. The noble lord, who, in a party attack on the most illustrious of his countrymen, told the House of Commons that one of the Clerks of Session wrote more books than any other person had leisure to read, would probably have accomplished an unusual feat if he had read in one day the forty pages 8vo. which Scott sometimes wrote in the same period of time. We find that the two sermons which Scott wrote for a clerical friend were promised overnight and placed in his hand the next morning. The absence of apparent effort in the exercise of even his highest powers struck all strangers who had an opportunity of observing his talents. Two acute, and by no means superstitious observers, solved the mystery by ascribing to him something of supernatural power. " There was," says Hazlitt, "a degree of capacity in that huge double forehead which superseded all effort, and made everything come intuitively and almost

E.   6

.nechanically." Captain Basil Hall was at first much exercised by the phenomena, but as he himself kept a very copious journal, and discovered that in one of his visits to Abbotsford he had written in one day about as much as Scott considered a fair day's task, he considered that his wonder was misapplied. "No such great matter after all," concluded the gallant captain; "it is mere industry and a little invention, and that we all know costs Scott nothing." (A laugh.) In fact, amongst his intimate friends the marvellous facility and fecundity of the man ceased to excite any surprise. Even the faithful and affectionate Laidlaw, his amanuensis in times of sickness, used to forget himself and everything else in the interest of the tale he was writing down. If the dictation flagged, he would say, "Come, sir, get on; get on"; and would receive the characteristic reply, "Hout! Willie, you forget I have to invent the story!" (Laughter.)

It is natural at first sight to regret all this headlong haste, and to wish that four or five of the novels had been compressed into a perfect work of art, into a "gem of purest ray serene" altogether worthy of the mind whence it came. No doubt, the rule of Goldsmith's connoisseur is generally a sound one, that the picture would have been better had the painter taken more pains; and if we can conceive such a thing as a pedagogue seated with a row of possible Walter Scotts before him, it would be highly proper that he should impress the maxim on their young minds. But as the genius of Scott was in so many points exceptional, it is possible that it may have worked under special laws of his own, and that something of the charm of his works may belong to their rapid and spontaneous flow, like the rush of a river, or the melody from the throats of birds

"That carol their secret pleasures to the spring."

From a Speech delivered by Sir William Stirling-Maxwell at the Centenary of Sir Walter Scott.

50

Thus, then, you have first to mould her physical frame, and then, as the strength she gains will permit you, to fill and temper her mind with all knowledge and thoughts which tend to confirm its natural instincts of justice, and refine its natural tact of love.

All such knowledge should be given her as may enable her to understand, and even to aid, the work of men : and yet it should be given, not as a knowledge,—not as if it were, or could be, for her an object to know ; but only to feel, and to judge.

It is of no moment, as a matter of pride or perfectness in herself, whether she knows many languages or one ; but it is of the utmost that she should be able to show kindness to a stranger, and to understand the sweetness of a stranger's tongue. It is of no moment to her own worth or dignity that she should be acquainted with this science or that ; but it is of the highest that she should be trained in habits of accurate thought, that she should understand the meaning, the inevitableness, and the loveliness of natural laws ; and follow at least some one path of scientific attainment, as far as to the threshold of that bitter Valley of Humiliation, into which only the wisest and bravest of men can descend, owning themselves for ever children, gathering pebbles on a boundless shore. It is of little consequence how many positions of cities she knows, or how many dates of events, or names of celebrated persons—it is not the object of education to turn the woman into a dictionary ; but it is deeply necessary that she should be taught to enter with her whole personality into the history she reads ; to picture the passages of it vitally in her own bright imagination ; to apprehend, with her fine instincts, the pathetic circumstances and dramatic relations, which the historian too often only eclipses by his reasoning, and disconnects by his arrangement : it is for her to trace the hidden equities of divine reward, and catch sight, through the darkness, of the fateful threads of woven fire that connect error with retribution. But, chiefly of all, she is to be taught to extend the limits of her sympathy with respect to that history which is being for ever determined as the moments pass in which she draws her peaceful breath ; and to the contemporary calamity, which, were it but rightly mourned by her, would recur no more hereafter. She is to exercise herself in imagining what would be the effects upon her mind and conduct, if she were daily brought into the presence of the suffering which is not the less real because shut from her sight. She is to be taught somewhat to understand the nothingness of the proportion which that little world in which she lives and loves bears to the world in which God lives and loves ;—and solemnly she is to be taught to strive that her thoughts of piety may not be feeble in proportion to the number they embrace, nor her prayer more languid than it is for the momentary relief from pain of her husband or her child, when it is uttered for the multitudes of those who have none to love them,—and is "for all who are desolate and oppressed."

RUSKIN, *Sesame and Lilies.*

51

There is something in the character and habits of the North American savage, taken in connection with the scenery over which he is accustomed to range, its vast lakes, boundless forests, majestic rivers, and trackless plains, that is to my mind wonderfully striking and sublime. He is formed for the wilderness, as the Arab is for the desert. His nature is stern, simple, and enduring; fitted to grapple with difficulties and to support privations. There seems but little soil in his heart for the support of the kindly virtues ; and yet, if we would but take the trouble to penetrate through that proud stoicism and habitual taciturnity, which lock up his character from casual observation, we should find him linked to his fellow man of civilized life by more of those sympathies and affections than are usually ascribed to him.

It has been the lot of the unfortunate aborigines of America, in the early periods of colonization, to be doubly wronged by the white men. They have been dispossessed of their hereditary possessions by mercenary and frequently wanton warfare; and their characters have been traduced by bigoted and interested writers. The colonist often treated them like beasts of the forest; and the author has endeavoured to justify him in his outrages. The former found it easier to exterminate than to civilize; the latter to vilify than to discriminate. The appellations of savage and pagan were deemed sufficient to sanction the hostilities of both; and thus the poor wanderers of the forest were persecuted and defamed, not because they were guilty, but because they were ignorant.

The rights of the savage have seldom been properly appreciated or respected by the white man. In peace he has too often been the dupe of artful traffic; in war he has been regarded as a ferocious animal, whose life or death was a question of mere precaution and convenience. Man is cruelly wasteful of life when his own safety is endangered, and he is sheltered by impunity; and little mercy is to be expected from him, when he feels the sting of the reptile, and is conscious of the power to destroy.

The same prejudices which were indulged thus early exist in common circulation at the present day.

The current opinion of the Indian character, however, is too apt to be formed from the miserable hordes which infest the frontiers, and hang on the skirts of the settlements. These are too commonly composed of degenerate beings, corrupted and enfeebled by the vices of society, without being benefited by its civilization. That proud independence which formed the main pillar of savage virtue, has been shaken down, and the whole moral fabric lies in ruins. Their spirits are humiliated and debased by a sense of inferiority, and their native courage cowed and daunted by the superior knowledge and power of their enlightened neighbours. Society has advanced upon them like one of those withering airs, that will sometimes breed desolation over a whole region of fertility. It has enervated their strength, multiplied their diseases, and superinduced upon their original barbarity the low vices of artificial life. It has given them a thousand superfluous wants, whilst it has diminished their means of mere existence. It has driven before it the animals of the chase, who fly from the sound of the axe and the smoke of the settlement, and seek refuge in the depths of the remotest forests and yet untrodden wilds. Thus do we too often find the Indians on our frontiers to be the mere wrecks and remnants of once powerful tribes, who have lingered in the vicinity of the settlements, and sunk into precarious and vagabond existence. Poverty, repining and hopeless poverty, a canker of the mind unknown in savage life, corrodes their spirits and blights every free and noble quality of their natures. They become drunken, indolent, feeble, thievish, and pusillanimous. They loiter like vagrants about the settlements, among spacious dwellings replete with elaborate comforts which only render them sensible of the comparative wretchedness of their own condition. Luxury spreads its ample board before their eyes; but they are excluded from the banquet. Plenty revels over the fields; but they are starving in the midst of its abundance; the whole wilderness has blossomed into a garden; but they feel as reptiles that infest it. WASHINGTON IRVING (abridged).

52

It has always been reckoned among the most difficult problems in the practical science of government, to combine an hereditary monarchy with security of freedom, so that neither the ambition of kings shall undermine the people's rights, nor the jealousy of the people over-turn the throne. England had already experience of both these mischiefs. And there seemed no prospect before her but either their alternate recurrence or a final submission to absolute power, unless by one great effort she could put the monarchy for ever beneath the law, and reduce it to an integrant portion instead of the primary source and principle of the Constitution. She must reverse the favoured maxim, "A Deo rex, a rege lex"; and make the Crown itself appear the creature of the law. But our ancient monarchy, strong in a possession of seven centuries, and in those high and paramount prerogatives which the consenting testimony of lawyers and the submission of

Parliaments had recognised—a monarchy from which the House
of Commons and every existing peer, though not perhaps the
aristocratic order itself, derived its participation in the legislative
—could not be bent to the republican theories which have been
not very successfully attempted in some modern codes of constitution. It could not be held, without breaking up all the
foundations of our polity, that the monarchy emanated from the
Parliament, or even from the people. But by the Revolution
and by the Act of Settlement, the rights of the actual monarch,
of the reigning family, were made to emanate from the Parliament
and the People. In technical language, in the grave and
respectful theory of our Constitution, the Crown is still the
fountain from which law and justice spring forth. Its prerogatives are in the main the same as under the Tudors and
the Stuarts; but the right of the House of Brunswick to exercise
them can only be deduced from the Convention of 1688.

The great advantage, therefore, of the Revolution, as I would
explicitly affirm, consists in that which was reckoned its reproach
by many, and its misfortune by more, that it broke the line of
succession. No other remedy could have been found, according
to the temper and prejudices of those times, against the unceasing
conspiracy of power. But when the very tenure of power was
conditional, when the Crown, as we may say, gave recognizances
for its good behaviour, when any violent and concerted aggressions
on public liberty would have ruined those who could only resist
an inveterate faction by the arms which liberty put in their hands,
the several parts of the Constitution were kept in cohesion by a
tie far stronger than statutes, that of a common interest in its
preservation. The attachment of James to Popery, his infatuation,
his obstinacy, his pusillanimity, nay, even the death of the Duke
of Gloucester, the life of the Prince of Wales, the extraordinary
permanence and fidelity of his party, were all the destined means
through which our present grandeur and liberty, our dignity of
thinking on matters of government, have been perfected. Those
liberal tenets, which at the era of the Revolution were maintained
but by one denomination of English party, and rather perhaps on

authority of not very good precedents in our history than of sound general reasoning, became in the course of the next generation almost equally the creed of the other, whose long exclusion from government taught them to solicit the people's favour; and by the time that Jacobitism was extinguished, had passed into received maxims of English politics. None at least would care to call them in question within the walls of Parliament; nor have their opponents been of much credit in the paths of literature.

HALLAM, *Constitutional History.*

53

The state of anarchy and confusion, into which has fallen the whole realm of relief and assistance to the poor and to persons in distress, is so generally recognised that many plans of reform have been submitted to us, each representing a section of public opinion. In fact throughout the three years of our investigations, we have been living under a continuous pressure for a remodelling of the Poor Laws and the Unemployed Workmen Act, in one direction or another. We do not regret this peremptory and insistent demand for reform. The present position is, in our opinion, as grave as that of 1834, though in its own way. We have, on the one hand, in England and Wales, Scotland and Ireland alike, the well-established Destitution Authorities, under ineffective central control, each pursuing its own policy in its own way; sometimes rigidly restricting its relief to persons actually destitute, and giving it in the most deterrent and humiliating forms; sometimes launching out into an indiscriminate and unconditional subsidising of mere poverty; sometimes developing costly and palatial institutions for the treatment, either gratuitously or for partial payment, of practically any applicant of the wage-earning or of the lower middle class. On the other hand, we see existing, equally ubiquitous with the Destitution Authorities, the newer specialised organs of Local Government—the Local Education Authority, the Local Health Authority, the Local

Lunacy Authority, the Local Unemployment Authority, the Local Pension Authority—all attempting to provide for the needs of the poor, according to the cause or character of their distress. Every Parliamentary Session adds to the powers of these specialised Local Authorities. Every Royal Commission or Departmental Committee recommends some fresh development of their activities. Thus, even while our Commission has been at work, a Departmental Committee has reported in favour of handing over the Vagrants, and what used to be called the "Houseless Poor," to the Local Police Authority, as being interested in "Vagrancy as a Whole," apart from the accident of a Vagrant being destitute. The Royal Commission on the Care and Control of the Feeble-minded has recommended that all mentally defective persons now maintained by the Poor Law should be handed over to the Local Authority specially concerned with mental deficiency, whether in a destitute or in a non-destitute person. The increasing activities of these specialised Local Authorities, being only half-consciously sanctioned by public opinion, and only imperfectly authorised by statute, are spasmodic and uneven. Whilst, for instance, the Local Education Authorities, and the Local Health Authorities are providing in some places gratuitous maintenance and medical treatment for one set of persons after another, similar Authorities are rigidly confining themselves to the bare fulfilment of their statutory obligations of schooling and sanitation. Athwart the overlapping and rivalry of these half-a-dozen Local Authorities that may be all at work in a single district, we watch the growing stream of private charity and voluntary agencies—the alms-houses and pensions for the aged; hospitals and dispensaries, convalescent homes and "medical missions" for the sick; free dinners and free boots, country holidays and "happy evenings" for the children; free shelters and soup kitchens, "way tickets," and charitable jobs for the able bodied, together with uncounted indiscriminate doles of every description—without systematic organisation and without any co-ordination with the multifarious forms of public activity. What the nation is confronted with today is, as it was in 1834, an evergrowing expenditure from public and private funds, which results, on the one hand, in a minimum of prevention and cure, and on the other in far-reaching demoralization of character and the continuance of no small amount of unrelieved destitution.

Poor Law Commission, Minority Report.

54

But although historically we are justified in saying that the first geometrician was a ploughman, the first botanist a gardener, the first mineralogist a miner, it may reasonably be objected that in this early stage a science is hardly a science yet; that measuring a field is not geometry, that growing cabbages is very far from botany, and that a butcher has no claim to the title of comparative anatomist. This is perfectly true; yet it is but right that each science should be reminded of these its more humble beginnings, and of the practical requirements which it was originally intended to answer. Now, although it may seem as if, in the present high state of our society, students were enabled to devote their time to the investigation of the facts and laws of nature, or to the contemplation of the mysteries of the world of thought, without any side glance at the practical results of their labours, no science and no art have long prospered and flourished among us, unless they were in some way subservient to the practical interests of society. It is true that a Lyell collects and arranges, a Faraday weighs and analyses, an Owen dissects and compares, a Herschel observes and calculates, without any thought of the immediate marketable results of their labours. But there is a general interest which supports and enlivens their researches, and that interest depends upon the practical advantages that society at large derives from these scientific studies. Let it be known that the successive strata of the geologist are a deception to the miner, that the astronomical tables are useless to the navigator, that chemistry is but an expensive amusement, of no use to the manufacturer and the farmer—and astronomy, chemistry, and geology would soon share the fate of alchemy and astrology. As long as alchemy instigated the avarice of its patrons by the promise of the discovery of gold, it prepared the way to discoveries more valuable. The same with astrology. Astrology was not such mere imposition as it is generally supposed to have been. Even Bacon allows it a place among the sciences, though admitting that "it had better intelligence and confederacy with the imagination of man than with his reason." In spite of the strong condemnation which Luther pronounced against it, astrology continued to sway the destinies of Europe, and a hundred years after Luther, the astrologer was the counsellor of princes and generals, while the founder of modern astronomy died in poverty and despair. In our time the very rudiments of astrology are lost and forgotten. Even real and useful arts, as soon as they cease to be useful, die away and their secrets are sometimes lost beyond the hope of recovery. When after the Reformation our churches and chapels were divested of their artistic ornaments in order to restore in outward appearance also the simplicity and purity of the Christian church, the colours of the painted windows began to fade away, and have never regained their former depth and harmony. The invention of printing gave the death-blow to the art of ornamental writing and of miniature painting employed in the illumination of manuscripts; and the best artists of the present day despair of rivalling the minuteness, softness, and brilliancy combined by the humble manufacturer of the mediaeval missal.

London Matriculation, September 12th, 1910.

55

So far from the position holding true, that great wit (or genius, in our modern way of speaking) has a necessary alliance with insanity, the greatest wits, on the contrary, will ever be found to be the sanest writers. It is impossible for the mind to conceive a mad Shakespeare. The greatness of wit, by which the poetic talent is here chiefly to be understood, manifests itself in the

admirable balance of all the faculties. Madness is the dispro-
portionate straining or excess of any one of them. "So strong a
wit," says Cowley, speaking of a poetical friend,

> "...... did Nature to him frame,
> As all things but his judgment overcame;
> His judgment like the heavenly moon did show,
> Tempering that mighty sea below."

The ground of the mistake is, that men, finding in the raptures
of the higher poetry a condition of exaltation, to which they have
no parallel in their own experience, besides the spurious resemblance of it in dreams and fevers, impute a state of dreaminess
and fever to the poet. But the true poet dreams being awake.
He is not possessed by his subject, but has dominion over it. In
the groves of Eden he walks familiar as in his native paths. He
ascends the empyrean heaven, and is not intoxicated. He treads
the burning marl without dismay; he wins his flight without self-
loss through realms "of chaos and old night." Or if, abandoning
himself to that severer chaos of a "human mind untuned," he is
content awhile to be mad with Lear, or to hate mankind (a sort
of madness) with Timon, neither is that madness, nor this mis-
anthropy, so unchecked, but that,—never letting the reins of
reason wholly go, while most he seems to do so,—he has his
better genius still whispering at his ear, with the good servant
Kent suggesting saner counsels, or with the honest steward Flavius
recommending kindlier resolutions. Where he seems most to
recede from humanity, he will be found the truest to it. From
beyond the scope of Nature if he summon possible existences, he
subjugates them to the law of her consistency. He is beautifully
loyal to that sovereign directress, even when he appears most to
betray and desert her. His ideal tribes submit to policy; his
very monsters are tamed to his hand, even as that wild sea-brood
shepherded by Proteus. He tames, and he clothes them with
attributes of flesh and blood, till they wonder at themselves, like
Indian Islanders forced to submit to European vesture. Caliban,
the Witches, are as true to the laws of their own nature (ours with

93

a difference), as Othello, Hamlet, and Macbeth. Herein the great
and the little wits are differenced; that if the latter wander ever
so little from nature or actual existence, they lose themselves, and
their readers. Their phantoms are lawless; their visions night-
mares. They do not create, which implies shaping and consistency.
Their imaginations are not active—for to be active is to call
something into act and form—but passive, as men in sick dreams.
For the super-natural, or something super-added to what we know
of nature, they give you the plainly non-natural. And if this were
all, and that these mental hallucinations were discoverable only
in the treatment of subjects out of nature, or transcending it, the
judgment might with some plea be pardoned if it ran riot, and
a little wantonized: but even in the describing of real and every-
day life, that which is before their eyes, one of these lesser wits
shall more deviate from nature—show more of that inconsequence,
which has a natural alliance with frenzy, than a great genius in
his "maddest fits," as Wither somewhere calls them.

CHARLES LAMB, *The last Essays of Elia.*

56

And first, truly, to all them that, professing learning, inveigh
against poetry may justly be objected, that they go very near to
ungratefulness, to seek to deface that which, in the noblest nations
and languages that are known, hath been the first light-giver to
ignorance, and first nurse, whose milk by little and little enabled
them to feed afterwards of tougher knowledges. And will you
play the hedgehog, that being received into the den, drove out
his host? or rather the vipers, that with their birth kill their
parents? Let learned Greece, in any of her manifold sciences,
be able to show me one book before Musaeus, Homer, and Hesiod,
all three nothing else but poets. Nay, let any history be brought,
that can say any writers were there before them, if they were not
men of the same skill, as Orpheus, Linus, and some others are
named, who, having been the first of that country that made pens
deliverers of their knowledge to posterity, may justly challenge

to be called their fathers in learning. For not only in time they had this priority, (although in itself antiquity be venerable,) but went before them as causes, to draw with their charming sweetness the wild untamed wits to an admiration of knowledge. So as Amphion was said to move stones with his poetry to build Thebes, and Orpheus to be listened to by beasts, indeed stony and beastly people; so among the Romans were Livius Andronicus, and Ennius: so in the Italian language, the first that made it to aspire to be a treasure-house of science, were the poets Dante, Boccace, and Petrarch: so in our English were Gower and Chaucer; after whom, encouraged and delighted with their excellent foregoing, others have followed to beautify our mother-tongue, as well in the same kind, as other arts. This did so notably show itself, that the philosophers of Greece durst not a long time appear to the world, but under the mask of poets: so Thales, Empedocles, and Parmenides, sang their natural philosophy in verses: so did Tyrtaeus in war matters, and Solon in matters of policy: or rather they being poets, did exercise their delightful vein in those points of highest knowledge, which before them lay hidden to the world; for that wise Solon was directly a poet it is manifest, having written in verse the whole fable of the Atlantic Island, which was continued by Plato. And, truly, even Plato, whosoever well considereth, shall find that in the body of his work, though the inside and strength were philosophy, the skin, as it were, and beauty, depended most of poetry. For all stands upon dialogues, wherein he feigns many honest burgesses of Athens to speak of such matters, that if they had been set on the rack they would never have confessed them; besides his poetical describing the circumstances of their meetings, as the well-ordering of a banquet, the delicacy of a walk, with interlacing mere tales, as Gyges's Ring, and others; which who knows not to be flowers of poetry, did never walk into Apollo's garden. And even historiographers, although their lips sound of things done and verity be written in their foreheads, have been glad to borrow, both fashion, and, perchance, weight, of the poets: so Herodotus intituled his history by the names of the Nine Muses; and both he, and all the rest that followed him, either stole or usurped, of poetry, their passionate describing of passions, the many particularities of battles which no man could affirm ; or, if that be denied me, long orations, put in the mouths of great kings and captains, which it is certain they never pronounced. So that, truly, neither philosopher nor historiographer could, at the first, have entered into the gates of popular judgment, if they had not taken a great passport of poetry : which in all nations, at this day, where learning flourisheth not, is plain to be seen ; in all which they have some feeling of poetry.

SIDNEY, *Defence of Poesie.*

57

THE FOREST OF ARDEN.

Enter DUKE *Senior,* AMIENS, *and other* LORDS, *like Foresters.*

Duke S. Now, my co-mates and brothers in exile,
Hath not old custom made this life more sweet
Than that of painted pomp? Are not these woods
More free from peril than the envious court?
Here feel we but the penalty of Adam,
The season's difference ; as, the icy fang,
And churlish chiding of the winter's wind,
Which, when it bites and blows upon my body,
Even till I shrink with cold, I smile and say
"This is no flattery : these are counsellors
That feelingly persuade me what I am."
Sweet are the uses of adversity,
Which, like the toad, ugly and venomous,
Wears yet a precious jewel in his head ;
And this our life exempt from public haunt
Finds tongues in trees, books in the running brooks,
Sermons in stones and good in everything.
I would not change it.

Ami.   Happy is your grace,
That can translate the stubbornness of fortune
Into so quiet and so sweet a style.
Duke S. Come, shall we go and kill us venison?
And yet it irks me the poor dappled fools,
Being native burghers of this desert city,
Should in their own confines with forked heads
Have their round haunches gored.
First Lord.   Indeed, my lord,
The melancholy Jaques grieves at that;
And, in that kind, swears you do more usurp
Than doth your brother that hath banish'd you.
To-day, my Lord of Amiens and myself
Did steal behind him as he lay along
Under an oak whose antique root peeps out
Upon the brook that brawls along this wood:
To the which place a poor sequester'd stag,
That from the hunter's aim had ta'en a hurt,
Did come to languish, and indeed, my lord,
The wretched animal heaved forth such groans
That their discharge did stretch his leathern coat
Almost to bursting, and the big round tears
Coursed one another down his innocent nose
In piteous chase; and thus the hairy fool,
Much marked of the melancholy Jaques,
Stood on the extremest verge of the swift brook,
Augmenting it with tears.
Duke S.   But what said Jaques?
Did he not moralize this spectacle?
First L.   O, yes, into a thousand similes.
First, for his weeping into the needless stream;
"Poor deer," quoth he, "thou mak'st a testament
As worldlings do, giving thy sum of more
To that which had too much": then, being there alone,
Left and abandon'd of his velvet friends,
"'Tis right": quoth he; "thus misery doth part

The flux of company ": anon, a careless herd,
Full of the pasture, jumps along by him
And never stays to greet him; "Ay," quoth Jaques,
"Sweep on, you fat and greasy citizens;
'Tis just the fashion: wherefore do you look
Upon that poor and broken bankrupt there?"
Thus most invectively he pierceth through
The body of the country, city, court,
Yea, and of this our life, swearing that we
Are mere usurpers, tyrants and what's worse,
To fright the animals and to kill them up
In their assign'd and native dwelling-place.

Duke S. And did you leave him in this contemplation?

Sec. Lord. We did, my lord, weeping and commenting
Upon the sobbing deer.

Duke S.   Show me the place:
I love to cope him in these sullen fits,
For then he's full of matter.

First Lord.   I'll bring you to him straight.

SHAKESPEARE, *As You Like It.*

53

In every species of creatures, those who have been least time
in the world appear best pleased with their condition; for, besides
that to a new comer the world hath a freshness on it that strikes
the sense after a most agreeable manner, being itself, unattended
with any great variety of enjoyments, excites a sensation of
pleasure. But as age advances, everything seems to wither, the
senses are disgusted with their old entertainments, and existence
turns flat and insipid. We may see this exemplified in mankind;
the child, let him be free from pain and gratified in his change
of toys, is diverted with the smallest trifle. Nothing disturbs the
mirth of the boy but a little punishment or confinement. The
youth must have more violent pleasures to employ his time; the
man loves the hurry of an active life, devoted to the pursuits of

wealth or ambition; and lastly, old age, having lost its capacity for these avocations, becomes its own insupportable burden. This variety may in part be accounted for by the vivacity and decay of the faculties; but I believe is chiefly owing to this, that the longer we have been in possession of being, the less sensible is the gust we have of it; and the more it requires of adventitious amusements to relieve us from the satiety and weariness it brings along with it.

And as novelty is of a very powerful, so it is of a most extensive influence. Moralists have long since observed it to be the source of admiration, which lessens in proportion to our familiarity with objects, and upon a thorough acquaintance is utterly extinguished. But I think it hath not been so commonly remarked, that all the other passions depend considerably on the same circumstances. What is it but novelty that awakens desire, enhances delight, kindles anger, provokes envy, inspires horror? To this cause we must ascribe it that love languishes with fruition, and friendship itself is recommended by intervals of absence; hence monsters, by use, are beheld without loathing, and the most enchanting beauty without rapture. That emotion of the spirits in which passion consists is usually the effect of surprise, and as long as it continues, heightens the agreeable or disagreeable qualities of its object; but as this emotion ceases (and it ceases with the novelty), things appear in another light, and affect us even less than might be expected from their proper energy, for having moved us too much before.

It may not be an useless enquiry how far the love of novelty is the unavoidable growth of nature, and in what respects it is peculiarly adapted to the present state. To me it seems impossible that a reasonable creature should rest absolutely satisfied in any acquisition whatever, without endeavouring farther; for after its highest improvements, the mind hath an idea of an infinity of things still behind worth knowing, to the knowledge of which therefore it cannot be indifferent; as by climbing up a hill in the midst of a wide plain a man hath his prospects enlarged, and, together with that, the bounds of his desires. Upon this account, I cannot think he detracts from the state of the blessed, who conceives them to be perpetually employed in fresh searches into nature, and to eternity advancing into the fathomless depths of the divine perfections.

London Matriculation, September 14th, 1908.

59

Here Adeimantus interposed, inquiring, "Then what defence will you make, Socrates, if anyone protests that you are not making the men of this class particularly happy?—when it is their own fault, too, if they are not; for the city really belongs to them, and yet they derive no advantage from it, as others do, who own lands, and build fine large houses, and furnish them in corresponding style, and perform private sacrifices to the gods, and entertain their friends, and, in fact, as you said just now, possess gold and silver, and everything that is usually considered necessary to happiness; nay, they appear to be posted in the city, as it might be said, precisely like mercenary troops, wholly occupied in garrison duties."

"Yes," I said, "and for this they are only fed, and do not receive pay in addition to their rations, like the rest, so that it will be out of their power to take any journeys on their own account, should they wish to do so, or to lay out money in the gratification of any other desire, after the plan of those who are considered happy. These and many similar counts you leave out of the indictment."

"Well," said he, "let us suppose these to be included in the charge."

"What defence then shall we make, say you?"

"Yes."

"By travelling the same road as before, we shall find, I think, what to say. We shall reply that, though it would not surprise us, if even this class in the given circumstances were very happy, yet that our object in the construction of our state is not to make any one class pre-eminently happy, but to make the whole state as happy as it can be made. For we thought that in such a state we should be most likely to discover justice, as, on the other hand, in the worst-regulated state we should be most likely to discover injustice, and that after having observed them we might decide the question we have been so long investigating. At present, we believe we are forming the happy state, not by selecting a few of its members and making them happy, but by making the whole so. Presently we shall examine a state of the opposite kind. Now, if some one came up to us while we were painting statues and blamed us for not putting the most beautiful colours on the most beautiful parts of the body, because the eyes, being the most beautiful part, were not painted purple, but black, we should think it a sufficient defence to reply, Pray, sir, do not suppose that we ought to make the eyes so beautiful as not to look like eyes, nor the other parts in like manner, but observe whether, by giving to every part what properly belongs to it, we make the whole beautiful. In the same way do not, in the present instance, compel us to attach to our guardians such a species of happiness as shall make them anything but guardians. For we are well aware that we might, on the same principle, clothe our cultivators in long robes, and put golden coronets on their heads, and bid them till the land at their pleasure; and that we might stretch our potters at their ease on couches before the fire, to drink and make merry, placing the wheel by their side, with directions to ply their trade just so far as they should feel it agreeable; and that we might dispense this kind of bliss to all the rest, so that the entire city might thus be happy. But give not such advice to *us*: since, if we comply with your recommendation, the cultivator will be no cultivator, the potter no potter; nor will any of those professions, which make up a state, maintain its proper character. For the other occupations it matters less; for in cobblers, incompetency and degeneracy and pretence without the reality, are not dangerous to a state: but when guardians of the laws and of the state are such in appearance only, and not in reality, you see that they radically destroy the whole state, as, on the other hand, they alone can create public prosperity and happiness. If then, while *we* aim at making genuine guardians, who shall be as far as possible from doing mischief to the state, the supposed objector makes a class who would be cultivators and as it were jovial feasters at a holiday gathering, rather than citizens of a state, he will be describing something which is not a state. We should examine then whether our object in constituting our guardians should be to secure to them the greatest possible amount of happiness, or whether our duty, as regards happiness, is to see if our state as a whole enjoys it, persuading or compelling these our auxiliaries and guardians to study only how to make themselves the best possible workmen at their own occupation, and treating all the rest in like manner, and thus, while the whole city grows and becomes prosperously organized, permitting each class to partake of as much happiness as the nature of the case allows to it."

PLATO, *Republic.* Davies and Vaughan's Translation.

60

In the industrial unrest of 1911-12 nothing caused more disquiet to the onlooker and to the business world than the tendency which appeared here and there among trade unionists to repudiate leaders and to disregard agreements. The whole position of collective bargaining gradually built up by workmen in the teeth of public opinion, and of late years accepted by employers as the best method after all of conducting industry on the great scale, seemed to be undermined. There were calls for the repeal of the Trade Disputes Act, and for the establishment of compulsory arbitration or some other heroic method of keeping the peace. One outcome of the agitation was that the Industrial Council was requested to inquire into the question of the maintenance of agreements, and at the same time into the allied question of the enforcement of agreements upon the non-unionist employer and workman. The Report, issued on Thursday, of this representative body of great employers and leading trade unionists is a remarkable document, not for the originality of its proposals, but for the weighty endorsement of the general principle of collective bargaining, and the success with which—strikes and lock-outs notwithstanding—it is working for the organisation of industry. The alarmist views are altogether set aside. The great majority of agreements, testifies this representative body, are honourably kept. With regard to those that are not so kept, there is generally, on the same testimony, a perfectly intelligible reason for the breach. Collective bargains are not, the Report points out, precisely the same as contracts of service. They are not direct agreements between the employer and the workman. They are agreements between representatives of large numbers, which numbers often contain a strongly dissentient minority. Not seldom their terms contain something which one party is forced to accept by the event of the stricken field. They are like treaties imposed on a conquered State, and it is in human nature to seek the first opportunity of escape from such treaties. The representatives of the losing side make the best of it. But their followers will not in such cases feel the full force of a moral obligation compelling them to abide by the terms, if they see, or think they see, that the wheel of fortune has come round to their side, and that the chance has arisen of getting back what in their hearts they always held their own.

None the less, that collective agreements should provide a firm basis on which both sides can rely is obviously essential to collective bargaining. The whole position of trade unionism was threatened by some of the events of the strike period. Is there any mechanism by which the repetition of such a danger can be avoided? Many suggestions have been before the Industrial Council, many that are very plausible at first sight but that break down upon close analysis. What could be more reasonable, for instance, than compulsory arbitration? In international politics we all look to arbitration as the hope of the future. And if in international politics, why not in labour politics? How much more reasonable, instead of wasting energy, losing business, and causing turmoil by a trial of strength, to submit everything to the deliberate judgment of a thoroughly impartial and fully instructed tribunal. No doubt it would be reasonable if that tribunal possessed, first, the principles on which the dispute should be settled—that is, if there existed agreed rules as to the basis on which wages, hours, &c. ought to be fixed—and, secondly, the means of enforcing its decisions. At present no such tribunal could be equipped with either of these essentials of success, and the Council, therefore, repudiates compulsory arbitration. Then, again, if either party repudiates an agreement that it has made, how just that it should pay money compensation. Most just in appearance. When we look at it more closely it is seen to be easily enforceable on employers, difficult to enforce and of doubtful real justice if enforced on trade unions. What causes breach of agreements by trade unionists is that a section of the men who feel some grievance keenly resent, and from the first desire to repudiate, the settlement to which their leaders are driven. If they rebel, they are rebelling as much against the union as against the employers. Fine the union and you only weaken its authority so much the more, and encourage revolt, and possibly secession, and the formation of a new and sectional union. Much the same result occurs if the union is legally forbidden to give strike pay. Such a prohibition would be very difficult to enforce, and if enforced the probable result would be secession. On the whole, we are driven with the Council to the conclusion that no legal devices would be of avail. We can imagine the evolution of such a body as the Industrial Council itself into a kind of court which in the first instance would be, as it were, a court of honour, pronouncing not only on the merits of disputes but on the methods used by either party, and holding up to moral reprobation any departure from the rules of the game, and we can imagine the decisions of such a court gradually acquiring binding force. But any such evolution must be the work of time and of the growth of confidence. The result is not to be achieved by the short cuts of heroic legislation.

Thus for the maintenance of agreements the Council stands by voluntaryism, and trusts to moral force. It is twitted with inconsistency in some quarters for preferring compulsion in respect of the other question which it had before it—the extension of agreements to the whole of a trade. Compulsion may be good or bad, according to circumstances, and there is not the smallest inconsistency in maintaining that it is warranted by one set of circumstances and not by another. In many trades there is a partial but not complete organisation of employers and employed. A Board of Conciliation representing both parties so far as organised agree on a schedule of conditions. But outside them are a number of non-unionist workmen and non-federated employers who do not accept the same conditions. The collective bargain has fixed the wages of a certain grade of labour, say, at 30s. a week. The non-federated employer gets non-union workmen of the same grade, say, at 25s. Obviously he has an immediate advantage in competition, and it is to the interest not only of the workmen but of the federated employers to bring him into the fold, or at least to bring him up to the mark. Should the State give any assistance in thus generalising agreements which represent as a rule the best practice of the firms of highest standing and of the most skilled and competent men? The majority of the Council think that it should. They propose a plan by which the Board of Trade should appoint a competent authority to hold an inquiry into the nature of any such agreement, and, after hearing both sides, to give to it the force of law. To our minds the most questionable point in the recommendations of the Council on this head—from which, it should be borne in mind, some weighty names among the employers dissent—is the somewhat arbitrary position given to the Board of Trade. We should have thought that something modelled rather on the Wages Boards that exist in the lower grades of industry might be better suited in the case. The Board would then be summoned by the Board of Trade, but it would consist of representatives of employers and employed, both organised and unorganised, with an impartial chairman, if necessary. Its business would be to discuss the application of an agreement already made by the organised body to the whole of the trade. It would hear the views of those claiming an exceptional position, and it would have in the end the power to issue a determination, not necessarily in exact conformity with the original agreement but with such modifications, for example, as might be suited to the needs of an outlying or backward district. We can even conceive that such a mechanism might do much to forward the general organisation of industry and to secure that levelling up of conditions without which it is always difficult for the best employers to make a substantial advance in improving the position of their own work-people.

From *The Manchester Guardian.*

INDEX OF AUTHORS QUOTED

[The references are to pages]